A NEW SONG

LEADER'S GUIDE
For
SMALL GROUP STUDY

A NEW SONG

Our Journey Toward Healing

LEADER'S GUIDE
For
SMALL GROUP STUDY

SUSAN HABEGGER

In the midst of suffering,

When the hues that color our lives are dark,

When the melodies are in minor chords,

When our words search only for another way to express the pain,

When our vision sees all through a shadowy veil of obscurity,

We forget that . . .

Beauty Is.

Quietly woven around you in your pain, beauty is.

The heavens declare the glory and

The skies proclaim the work of The Creator's hands.

Day after day they pour forth speech;

Night after night they reveal knowledge.

They have no speech; they use no words;

No sound is heard from them.

Yet their voice goes out into all the earth;

Their words to the ends of the world.

Beauty has not been destroyed.

You will discover it once again, perhaps in the most unlikely places.

Beauty Is.

CONTENTS

Why Use *A New Song* For A Group Study?

As the writing of *A New Song* neared completion, it was read and used by pre-release small groups, and the response was remarkable. It brought to light the number of people who need a defined way to begin the conversation about hurt and healing—particularly in the church, where it seems this discussion is often set aside.

This avoidance by the church could happen for a variety of reasons:

- Maybe we assume people don't want to talk about or listen to personal problems as a part of their everyday conversations.
- Maybe we are afraid of what will be shared.
- Maybe we think these types of conversations should be reserved for professional counseling.
- Maybe we fear such discussions will detract from the positive messages we believe should be given in church.

Regardless of the reasons, many shared that they generally feel the absence of this type of conversation in the church. It is as if there is an unspoken expectation that our experiences of suffering are to be kept outside the doors of worship. There is the offer—and even the expectation—of healing, but aside from the random counseling referral, there is often little to no guidance in how to get there. There is no provision of a safe time and space where we can talk openly about the raw, unfiltered hurt that longs for healing.

This is where *A New Song* comes in. Innately built into this book for individuals going through suffering is a format that churches can work within to conduct safe, relevant, and organized conversations around this difficult topic.

And that's just what this book study is—*a conversation*. It is *not* a counseling course and should not be offered as group therapy. The author of the book is not a licensed counselor and, most likely, neither are the leaders who will facilitate the small-group discussions. Rather, it is a safe, organized, intentional opportunity for people to talk openly and productively about their experiences of suffering and their responses to the disappointments, loss, and trauma in their lives.

Along those lines, perhaps the main benefit of applying *A New Song* to a small-group study is that it provides guidance for that discussion—and in a group where people are faced with becoming vulnerable through sharing, this guidance provides a welcome safety net. Let me give you a couple examples.

Imagine starting a small group for sharing pain and then simply "winging it." The results could be disastrous and do more harm than good. All of us long to share our stories, including our painful ones, but without any guidance for this process, we often struggle. What should we share? And how much? How do we "deliver" our story? Often, we either share too much and feel uncomfortable because we can't move forward, or we close ourselves off, putting on the face we think others expect to see—the one that says, "Yes, I have problems, but I have everything under control."

Then, once pain is shared, we wonder what to do with it. How do we respond? Do we become a dumping ground for emotion? Do we make a list of ways to "set things right?" By providing guidance for this part of the journey, A New Song gives participants and leaders a space in which they can feel freedom to engage in safe, relevant sharing—and ultimately, to grow.

The guidance itself is neither a dictated path, with a checklist to mark our progress, nor a free-for-all, inviting everyone to share from whatever topic they choose. It does not promise a quick fix to people's problems. It also does not begin with the answer and then encourage people to fit their problems into that answer. Rather, the guidance in A New Song begins with the person. It allows individuals to give attention to their unique experiences of pain without accusation or expectation, and then gently lays down steppingstones of truth that pave a path toward healing—principles they can use to discover how to come to peace with the suffering of their past, present, and future.

In the group setting, the natural outgrowth of this focus on the person is the nurtured bond between people. There is the recognition that each person is on a unique journey. We know that group members will not face the same situations, feel the same emotions, or make the same choices —but they will have an opportunity to discover and embrace the similarities they encounter as they travel parts of the road together. And as they share the journey and are guided toward a common focus, their sense of companionship and togetherness will grow.

Finally, using A New Song in a small-group book study can further the opportunity for ministry. Sometimes, as believers, we hesitate to reveal the rawness of our pain and suffering. We feel the church should exemplify life at its fullest, presenting the image that "all is well." But perhaps, it is by our acknowledgment that all is *not* well that we open the door to an awareness of peace, courage, and moments of healing—and arrive at a place where we discover what it *means* for all to be well. It could be that, through this very openness to pain, we become true examples of what it looks like to live life at its fullest. And it is only this real and truthful journey toward healing that gives the opportunity for the display of God's provision and love, since it is He who journeys with us and helps us.

We don't need to be afraid to talk about suffering. It is one of our most common experiences. Our stories long to be told, and our hearts cry out to be heard. Our spirits yearn for the permission to express disquiet—followed by the gentle reminder that we have a reason for hope.

My desire, then, is that A New Song will provide church communities with . . .

- the encouragement to speak about pain openly and without fear;
- the foothold and assistance they need to come alongside those who long for a safe place—and companionship—to travel the path toward healing;
- the opportunity to introduce those experiencing pain to The Good Shepherd, our perfect Traveling Companion.

My hope is that, together, we can live out the following reality and help others to do the same:

> He put a new song in my mouth,
> a hymn of praise to our God.
> *Many will see* and fear the LORD
> *and put their trust in him.*
> —Psalm 40:3, emphasis mine

TESTIMONIES FROM
A NEW SONG
SMALL GROUP PARTICIPANTS

I wasn't sure what to expect from these sessions. I have heard so much about suffering and forgiveness. I have been told again and again to forget about my past. But my past was having a lot of impact on my present, so I just didn't understand how I could pretend that I wasn't going through what I was. Through *A New Song* sessions, I learned to acknowledge my suffering and be kind to myself. I learned that I don't have to let the suffering take over my life. I received a lot of clarity about myself. It was like meeting myself and hearing about my life. (Bangalore, India)

I felt that doing the time line and discussing it with my sisters in Christ really helped me move forward in facing my losses as well as my blessings. When we each shared in our small group there was a sense of compassion and courage that manifested itself—drawing us closer to one another— which was a real joy. (Sh. Denise Timbey Erie, CO)

I received answers to questions that I was afraid to ask. The sessions helped us learn how to stand firm on our own legs—and how to help others. (Lviv, Ukraine)

A large part of healing and comfort is in being understood. Through *A New Song* sessions I experienced an in-depth and true understanding of my suffering by someone who didn't know me at all, regarding things I had never shared with anyone. Truly Susan has passed on the comfort she received from God. (Bangalore, India)

A New Song sessions help those who are so confused and struggling with the chaos in their minds and hearts—it's like putting your messed up closet into order and sanity! (Bangalore, India)

Amazing wisdom and knowledge. Some one understands all the suffering I have gone through. Even when I couldn't understand me, or know how to articulate things, *A New Song* helped me process things better and understand trauma better! Blessings to you! (Tucson, AZ)

I admit that I was still looking back at the pain with my shoulders weighed down. Now I am able to accept the pain but look forward with hope. (Gulu, Uganda)

Arizona *A New Song* Life Group Participants:

I came angry, alone, and judged. I left hopeful, knowing I am not alone. I found forgiveness for myself.

I came as a little girl. I left as a big girl.

I came as a victim, feeling flat and monotone. I left open to embrace joy and rest.

I came despising suffering. I left seeing purpose, God's goodness, and hope within suffering.

I came discouraged and almost done. I left feeling hope, love, and seeing sun. The burdens are gone.

Others have come to help us. They tell us that everyone has suffered and we need to get over it. This one (*A New Song*) is different. This one connects with us in our pain. This one is touching my heart. (Gulu, Uganda)

A New Song sessions helped me to realize my internal hurt and how to find relief from that hurt. Suffering is not the whole story, but part of my life. I've learned that I can be held by God's love . . . I don't need to be carried away by the suffering. (Addis Ababa, Ethiopia)

I cannot say how much the course has meant to me. I realized that trauma was clouding my vision and I was seeing all of life through the trauma lens that I had put on over many years. There were many things that came alive. Even in the difficult things, the Lord led me to a place of quiet rest and acceptance. (Bangalore, India)

TESTIMONIES FROM
A NEW SONG
SMALL GROUP LEADERS

As a facilitator of *A New Song* small groups, I have witnessed the profound impact of Susan's teachings on many women. Susan's writing style fosters a sense of safety, belonging, and intimacy in group participants through shared healing experiences. This guide will give you practical help to lead a group on an authentic journey from suffering toward freedom and transformation.

Denisha Workizer, Founder & Executive Director of *Reclaimed Story*,
Trauma Survivor

The "A New Song" program was inaugurated at our parish to meet a great need. So many women had experienced traumatic experiences and felt they were alone in their struggles, each using precious energy to keep her head above water while feeling like she would never fully belong in community or be able to be herself because she couldn't share what had happened to her. The first thing *A New Song* did was to face that shame head on, healing it with grace. Participants learned that their responses to painful experiences were normal responses to trauma. They learned tools to help them begin to heal with God as their traveling companion on this road to wholeness. Small group sharing as part of the program encouraged bonding and the formation of a strong community of support. After *A New Song* finished at our parish, the small group portion grew into an active peer support group which continues to bring women together in healing from trauma. This is a program which meets the needs for healing and encourages spiritual growth for Christian women everywhere!

Sh. Margaret Ashton, Antiochian Women President,
St. Luke Orthodox Church, Erie, Colorado

Susan's interactive and transparent way of walking with leaders gives them the courage and tools to go from a hesitant walk to a confident run as they come alongside women during their healing journey.

Brianna Workman, Small Group Leader, Tucson, AZ

A New Song gently opens the door to the necessary conversations about pain and suffering that will provide a hope-filled way forward for those who desire peace and healing. Whether you are leading a group or participating as a fellow sojourner, Susan's thoughtful and compassionate language as well as her creative and insightful journaling activities provide an effective and encouraging path to follow that will lead to lasting healing.

Valerie L. McMahon, Author & Biblical Life Coach, Tucson , AZ

As a licensed counselor, I have used A New Song as sessions in my counseling practice with individuals and families. The information and tools have also been helpful to give further confidence to our professional and lay counselors in their work with those who experience trauma.

Mary Paul, Accredited Christian Counselor South Asia
Founder Director Vathsalya Charitable Trust, Founder Kutumba

A New Song has touched my life multiple times. First via zoom during covid which was also in the middle of my own trauma event. It was later when Susan visited India and taught portions of *A New Song* in person, that I began to realize that God was doing something with me which was more than my own healing—perhaps God was going to reach out to others through my own pain. Almost a year later I reached out to Susan, wondering if she would do the sessions again, but this time for a group of my friends from various locations in India and the U.K. via zoom. I am delighted for the book version of the course and my desire is that we will be a small group of women reading the book and meeting each week for a time of sharing and support. May the Lord lead us as we take these small steps, listening to Him and following Him into wholeness and abundant living.

Angel, Bangalore, India

A FEW RECOMMENDATIONS

FREQUENCY AND TIMING:

❋ This leader's guide divides the book into 12 sessions, providing a foundation from which you can develop a plan that best suits your intention and availability.

❋ Recommended time between sessions: 1-2 weeks.

> Experience has shown that 2 weeks is a long time between sessions. If a participant misses a session, it seems extremely long. 1-week intervals keep everyone on task and give the ability to share what is happening through the lessons without too much time passing.

> Avoid including too much in a session or moving too quickly. The gift of the journey will be lost if it feels like an assignment or a quick healing plan.

> Some groups provide 12 sessions, meeting every two weeks.

> Some groups provide 12 sessions, meeting every week.

> One group decided—after going through it once—to divide each session into two, and so spread the entire book over 24 weeks. This allows more sharing time and more careful attention to the focus for each reading.

❋ Recommended session time is 1.5 -2 hours.

GROUP LOGISTICS:

❋ Recommended small group size for sharing is 8-10.

❋ Preparation for each session includes assigned reading—multiple chapters—from the book. It can be helpful to give a suggested timeline for the reading. The time between sessions goes quickly and a quick read the evening before is not conducive to relevant sharing.

❋ Location for small group sharing should be separated and protected, away from areas where people are walking or congregating. If there is a perceived threat that others will hear, the group will not share freely. Experience has shown that multiple small groups in one room is disruptive. One group may be having an intense moment of sharing when another group enjoys a needed moment of laughter. In an instant, even with careful focus, a connection is broken and perhaps even a trigger is initiated.

❋ Gathering of people always includes socialization, especially as relationships grow. However, avoid allowing this small group time to become a social gathering. Start on time. End on time. Remember your intentions for the group.

* Experience has shown that refreshments are not necessary at this small group study. It is difficult to eat while sharing and listening, especially on personal and serious topics. It is an unneeded distraction and responsibility. The participants might appreciate availability of water, coffee, or tea. That being said, as the relationship grows, the group might want to meet informally—outside of the scheduled session time—over a meal or cup of coffee in order to spend more time together. This can be a lovely time of community.

GROUP DETAILS:

* Keep to the suggested topics of discussion. It may be tempting to open to "whatever is troubling you tonight." This can quickly lead down a path that actually hinders the progress of healing and destroys the intention for the group. The questions and topics for conversations have been carefully chosen to provide safe opportunities, along with boundaries, for telling our stories. When the conversation strays, gently bring it back. Feel confident in saying, "We are going to stick to the questions provided."

* Avoid referring to this as a counseling group. The book does not claim counseling credentials, nor does the author. The small group leaders are not intended or required to be counselors.

* If this group study is made up of multiple small groups within one larger group, a training session is recommended for all small group leaders. The guidance and reminders included in this guide are helpful—even when the leaders are seasoned and experienced. A New Song is not just another book study. We are not coming together to simply express *what we liked or what we found interesting*. This small group time is an opportunity perhaps long-awaited. The book is a foundation for the expression of story, of pain, of emotion. In a sense, it is not about the book as much as it is about the discovery of where the book takes each person.

It is helpful for all leaders to meet together for a time of preparation in order to be on the same page, coming from the same perspective and intention. This leaders guide can easily be used for the training.

LEADER GUIDANCE

Thank you for making the commitment to come alongside others in their search for healing, perhaps even as you make your own way forward. As you and your group take this journey of healing together, each of you will give attention to personal concerns, and yet, you will be able to share the experience together, providing encouragement and a witness for the individual stories told.

As such, note that this group is not a determination to link arms and pull each other along. Each person's journey is one-of-a-kind: we travel at different speeds, encounter different obstacles, and respond in different ways. In the group setting, however, each person will be able to glance around from where they are standing on the path and see familiar, compassionate faces.

Also note that this is not a "quick answer" study. We use the word *contemplative* often for good reason. To contemplate takes time and concentration. This word sets the tone for both the work at home and for the sharing time during each session.

Leading a group is a wonderful privilege but anticipating it can be overwhelming. Fortunately, preparation can help us feel less overwhelmed. The better prepared we are, the more smoothly we can navigate the unexpected things that can derail us as leaders and create instability in the group. A prepared and confident leader lays a safe, strong foundation for the participants. And that is the very purpose for this Leader's Guide—to prepare you to lead this small-group book study in the most effective way possible.

A LEADER'S MOTIVATION

We each have personal reasons for getting involved with those who suffer, but there is clearly biblical motivation to do this as well. God speaks compassionately about the oppressed and those who have been hurt, and He often intervenes to protect and walk with those who are suffering. We follow in Christ's footsteps when we come alongside the hurting. In fact, this is one of the ways we most bring glory to God and show His character—to humbly set ourselves aside in order to enter another person's place of pain, pointing to Jesus Christ as the ultimate Healer and Good Shepherd. This is what God has said about such an endeavor:

> You have been a refuge for the poor,
> a refuge for the needy in their distress, a shelter from the storm and a shade from the heat.
> For the breath of the ruthless is like a storm driving against a wall. (Isaiah 25:4)

A LEADER'S ROLE

In our role as leaders, it is important that we approach our group and its members with the correct intentions and mindset. This is especially important in groups such as this one, where difficult situations and emotions will be discussed, heightening people's sense of vulnerability. As such, here are a few key ideas to keep in mind as you enter the experience of leading a book-study group for *A New Song*:

* *A New Song* is here to come alongside people for an honest look at suffering. Your role in this is to create an atmosphere where participants feel safe enough for that to happen.

* Your role is to protect, encourage, and reassure. You will provide the stable ground that others need when they are feeling a bit shaky or precarious.

* Your role *is not* to fix people or their problems, or to get someone to the place you feel they should be. In this way, the leader of a group walks a difficult line, leading without directing.

* Avoid presenting the group or sessions as therapy or counseling time or referencing yourself as a counselor (unless, of course, you are a trained counselor using *A New Song* for counseling purposes).

* Inevitably, a bond will grow between you and the participants, but be careful not to encourage emotional or advisory dependence.

* You are the leader, but you are also part of the group. You are on this healing journey with the participants. As such, it is important that you do the assigned reading, not simply in preparation to lead but also as one on the journey. It is important that you, too, stop at the bends in the road, and not simply out of curiosity for how the participants will respond; rather, stop there and settle into a conversation with yourself. You don't want to miss this experience and what it can mean in your own life. Your own personal experience will add sweet depth and reality to your responses. Your vulnerability and genuineness will shine through as a fellow sojourner and guide on the journey rather than as a disconnected leader, concerned only with overseeing the progress of others.

A LEADER'S COMMITMENT

As leaders, we speak to the value of this study and to the perseverance of the participants through our own commitment. The safety of the group is established through consistency of action, expectation, and response:

* Commit to attend group sessions regularly. The participants will become accustomed to your guidance of the group, and your consistency will establish trust and safety. Frequent changes in leadership can be uncomfortable for the group. The feeling of safety is shaken with unexpected change.

* Commit to prepare the meeting area before each session, to make it a welcoming place. It is good to arrive before participants so that you can turn on lights, arrange seating, and clean up any messes that have been left. Your physical preparation speaks to the participants and sets a tone of your care for and value of them.

* Commit to keep everything that is shared by group members in confidence. Avoid "processing" with family, friends, or other leaders. By accepting this role, you commit to holding others' stories safe and protected.

  Note: There may be times when you want assistance from another leader about how to handle a particular experience or member in your group. In this case, it is acceptable to share about the situation as long as you keep names and details private. You could say, for example, "I have a participant who is finding it difficult to stay on topic and is giving long narrations of events in her life. How can I handle this situation in a way that is good for the entire group?" Or, "I have a participant who seems to need serious help with a particular event of suffering. How can I provide her with the support she needs?" It is also acceptable to ask a participant with a particular question or concern if you have their permission to seek guidance from someone outside the group.

* Commit to nurture an emotional environment that is safe. To *nurture* something is to care for it in such a way that it gets stronger and healthier. We nurture a safe emotional environment through our listening, our responses, and the boundaries we keep in place for all group participants.

A LEADER'S RESPONSIBILITIES AND CHALLENGES

LISTENING AND RESPONDING

This study is an opportunity to provide people with a safe space for sharing. One of the most important things we can do to nurture this safe space for participants is to listen and respond well. This might sound like an easy task. However, to listen correctly is actually hard work. We can be easily distracted from correct listening, and it's not unusual to find ourselves in the middle of a conversation, realizing we have forgotten how to do this "simple" task. In addition, we nurture the safe setting with our responses, both verbally and nonverbally.

Here are some basic principles about listening and responding that might act as good reminders:

* Listen with *eye contact*, giving the speaker your full attention. As you listen, think about what is being said. Avoid spending your "listening" time planning what you will do that evening or what you will say to the next person. Do not choose that moment to search for a pen or notebook or to whisper instructions to a fellow participant. As you listen, give your full "mind-attention" to what is being said.

* Avoid the quick inclination to reassure the person who is sharing. We often feel an urgency to respond or offer reassurance when people share difficult information. Our desire to "help" in this way can even sometimes lead us to interrupt, and we find that we are speaking over them. But

when we interrupt, we break the speaker's pattern of thought and give the impression that what we have to say is more important than what is being said. It is as if we are stepping on the speaker's words to get to a particular purpose that we feel is important. In our hurry to reassure, we give the impression that we have heard enough.

* Don't be afraid of silence. Sometimes a participant will take a long pause while sharing to collect their thoughts before they go on. That silence is okay. Often, when we fill that silence, we break the flow of sharing and sometimes even cause the conversation to go in a different direction.

* Offering short responses to participants who are sharing is enough. The following are some short responses you can give while the person is sharing:
  - a nod of the head
  - a smile or an encouraging look
  - a simple "yes," "hm-m-m," "uh-huh," or "you're doing well"

  The exception to this (and to the guideline about not interrupting) is when the speaker continues on and on and does not give any indication of coming to a close. In that case, you might need to make a comment that brings the sharing to a close for that time. You might say something like, "Mary, I can tell that you have much to share about this event. I want to hear more, so I am grateful that we will be spending more time together at our next session. But for now, we need to give others an opportunity to share. We all want to go away today having told a part of our story. Thank you again for trusting us enough to share."

* Avoid referring to stories about yourself as a response to participants. When a person is sharing about a painful experience, we often think it's reassuring to let them know that we have experienced something similar. There might come a time for such a connection, and this type of connection can sometimes be helpful. But especially in the beginning, people tend to be very protective of their own stories. An event that causes suffering is personal. The pain is personal. The loss is personal. So, when someone is sharing about that pain and loss and another person jumps in and begins to tell their story instead, it detracts from the original speaker's experience, and comparison begins. They might begin to wonder, "Is my story less traumatic?" Or, "Did they make a better choice?" When we share our own story as a response, we do not intend to create those difficulties for the other person, but it happens.

At some point, usually later on in the experience of walking through this together, you will have an opportunity to make a simple statement that expresses that you have experienced something similar. Perhaps something like, "Yes, the feeling of being betrayed by someone you love is painful. I remember that I felt great loss." Or "I hear what you are saying. At one point in my life, I didn't think I could go on."

As you make such a statement, avoid the urge to add "but"—as in, "but then I trusted God, and I gained strength," or "but I let the pain go, and now I am feeling so much better." Those types of responses do not so much encourage as create the expectation for that person to come to where you now are.

There will be other ways that your connection will be revealed as well. God will open doors to them at just the right moment—perhaps even in one-on-one situations outside of group time. But as the leader, you must ensure that your story always remains in the background. If not, the door becomes closed to the participant—and opened to you.

* Empathize with the speaker's feelings. To *empathize* is to share the feelings of another person by putting yourself in their place.

To empathize is *not* to say, "I know how you feel." Remember that we cannot *know* how a person feels. Even if we have been through the same experience, there are differences. We each look at an event from our own viewpoint, which is based on things like personality, upbringing, education, culture, and so on. This means each person will have unique feelings and emotions, even about the same event. To empathize is to look at an event from the other person's perspective. We won't be able to do it perfectly, but we can try to come as close as possible. We will come closest when we set aside our own viewpoint and expectations.

* Some words show that we are listening. Some words prove that we did not hear what the person said. Avoid the technique of repeating what the person said. This quickly gets annoying and sometimes we do not say it the way the person intended it. When this happens, they will not likely correct, but might hesitate to share in the same way again.

* Verbal responses are important. Our words can open the door to more sharing or close the door. One of the best things you can do is to simply think carefully before responding. If the moment is right for a particular response, it will still be there in a few seconds.

It can be difficult to know what to say to participants when they share about a difficult experience, and our first response is often just to say whatever we think will make the person feel better. So, we say things like,

- "You are going to be okay."
- "Everything will get better."
- "So many have felt the same way you do."
- "We know God has a plan."
- "I know exactly how you feel."
- "We know that all things work out for good."
- "Someday, you will understand why this happened. For now, just trust."

But when we really stop to think about these words, we realize that some may not be true and others are simply no help to someone who is in the midst of great pain.

So as you consider your responses, remember that this time is not about fixing. You are not expected to give the answer to the struggle. The participants will discover truth and help along the way. This time is simply a gift to express the suffering and find a path forward. That journey will take time. And at times, it might feel uncomfortable.

The following are a few examples of appropriate responses. There are many more! As time goes on, you will discover other similar responses that you can use. But perhaps, this will get you started:

- "Mary, thank you for trusting us enough to share those feelings."
- "I can tell that those were not easy things to share with us. Well done."
- "Thank you for sharing those feelings out loud. I'm sure some of us can connect with you."
- "Thank you for trusting us with part of your story."
- "I can see that this particular bend in the road really spoke to you."

If possible, make a natural connection to the particular way that a person has shared. For example, "That was something you did not expect in your life. Thank you for speaking it clearly to us." Don't be afraid to say, "That is a difficult situation. I don't have words that feel adequate to respond to your pain. Just know that we are so glad you are here with us." And remember, many times a simple "thank you" is enough, followed by an open invitation for another participant to share: "Who will follow Mary on this question?" As you continue through the sessions, listening and praying and preparing and becoming more confident, these types of simple natural responses will come more easily.

* Avoid talking too much. It is easy to get involved in giving a response and realize you don't know how to stop!

* You are not expected to give a perfect "spiritual" response. In a church or religious setting, it is tempting to always give a spiritual response: a verse, a spiritual principle or truth, an example from the Bible, or a personal experience of trust and healing. Avoid this tendency. Although the Bible is our foundation for guidance and hope, these responses begin to feel like quick answers or even an assignment or expectation. They send the message, *If you do this, all will be well.* Or, *If you do as I did, you will heal in the same way.* Truths will come naturally through the sessions. Allow the participants to discover them and then to affirm their own healing steps.

* A nonverbal response is one that does not use words, but certainly communicates to the speaker. While a person is talking, our facial expressions can actually change to show that we are listening. Those expressions can send messages that are encouraging or unhelpful and even discouraging. Yawning, frowning, and laughing inappropriately are just a few nonverbal expressions by a listener that would discourage the person who is speaking. A gentle smile, a look of sadness, a look of concern in your eyes, and even a genuine tear are all positive, encouraging nonverbal responses. You can also respond nonverbally by making eye contact, nodding to show that you understand or hear, or leaning forward.

* As you listen to a person's words, you are also "listening" to their nonverbal communication. You can tell a lot about a person's emotions by their facial expressions, hand movements, and body posture. Also note these signals in those who are listening. For example, watch for those who seem to want to share but have trouble initiating by raising a hand. All of this is part of "active listening."

❋   You are responsible for modeling good listening to the group and nudging them in the right direction, if needed. For example, if a participant jumps in with assurance and advice for the person who is sharing, this can feel demanding and uncomfortable for everyone, especially for the one sharing, who is now expected to *do* something. In this situation, be ready to redirect by saying something like, "We are so grateful for your sharing, Mary. Our hearts connect with your pain, and we so want to fix it. However, we know that we can't. So, for now we stand with you; we hold your story safe."

PROTECTING THE SAFE SPACE

One particular challenge leaders face is protecting the well-being and safety of the group. You must strike the delicate balance between giving freedom and setting boundaries.

To nurture this safe setting, you must begin by setting expectations for all people involved. From the very outset, clarify that you expect every member to offer respect, kindness, and confidentiality, and to listen as others speak. That way, each person knows that when it is their time to speak, this time will be protected.

After the first session, you must continue to remind everyone of the expected etiquette. You can do this before each sharing time by clearly speaking about at least one or two of the etiquette guidelines (outlined for you in the introduction of this Leader's Guide). If the group then does a good job of following the guidelines, you can reinforce and encourage this behavior by expressing gratitude. You might say something like, "Thank you so much for the respect you show each other as you listen and share. This has really become a safe place for all of us."

Even after laying this groundwork, however, you may face challenges. As a leader, you will encounter many different personalities and people who have various levels of familiarity with how to share and listen to personal details responsibly within a small-group setting. This means some participants will require more graceful guidance than others.

Some group members may need additional guidance in how to listen and respond to those who are sharing. As the protector of the safe setting, you should never allow a discussion where multiple participants begin to advise another. Remember—and remind the participants, as necessary—that the intention of this sharing time is to give people the opportunity to express a part of their stories in a safe place. The focus of the time is on getting the opportunity to *speak*—not on receiving responses or input. The goal is not to give advice or to share "how it worked for me in a similar situation." As mentioned, advice and quick answers like these will likely only discourage further sharing.

This is not to say that participants cannot respond at all. For example, validating responses like, "Thank you for sharing that," "I have felt a similar betrayal," and "I'm sorry that happened to you," are acceptable. However, the primary "responder" in the group will be you, the leader. You are the protector of this opportunity for people to bring their pain into the light without comparison, shame, or expectation.

On the other hand, some group members may need additional guidance following the etiquette for sharing. For instance, how do you respond to a participant who wants to share on every question or who wants to share too personally—perhaps with family details that are not appropriate? What do you do when the sharing goes off topic, following trails that can quickly divert and even unsettle the sharing time? Here are some ideas for how to handle these common sharing challenges.

- You may need to gently interrupt if the speaker veers off topic or shows no sign of stopping soon. You might say something like, "Mary, this topic really got you thinking in many directions. Before you go further, though, let's come back to the question. Is there a way that you can relate your story to this chapter's bend in the road? Was there a truth you discovered in these chapters that speaks to this struggle?"

- You might need to set a boundary if a participant is eager to share in response to every question: "Mary, I see you want to share on this question, as well. I'm going to ask you to wait for now, though, so that others who might want to share also have a chance. I'm sure you understand. Thank you so much."

- You might need to talk to a participant one-on-one outside of group time. "Mary, I need your help. I can see that you feel very comfortable sharing often and in detail. I am grateful you feel safe in this group. Unfortunately, some of the other participants do not have that level of comfortableness in sharing yet. So, I need your help in providing the opportunity for others to share. For the next session, if you could look at the questions for sharing and choose just one or two that relate to you. At the next session, focus on sharing in response just to those questions, and then we will give the time to others on the remaining questions."

- If a participant begins sharing too personally, perhaps with names or details that are not appropriate, you might say, "Please remember that we do not want to talk about people by name and in detail because we don't want to reveal details that we will regret later. Thank you so much for your help."

Usually, members will respond to your help and input and adjust for the good of the group. But some individuals may become frustrated and not want to return if they are not "given the floor" as often as they want. In these situations, it is possible to give grace while also ultimately maintaining that your role is to lead the group—for the good of the group. It is a loss when an entire group of people misses an opportunity to take the path of healing because one person takes over. Therefore, safety for the majority of the group is the responsibility of the leader—even when it is uncomfortable.

PROTECTING YOUR OWN MENTAL HEALTH

You might not expect it, but the stories of the group may affect your emotional health. If you are empathetic, you will feel the pain that is shared, and, in many ways, that pain may become a heavy burden. The apostle Paul speaks of this in 2 Corinthians. After experiencing beatings, shipwrecks, rejection, sleeplessness, and many other struggles, Paul says,

Besides everything else,
I face daily the pressure
of my concern for all the churches.
(2 Corinthians 11:28; emphasis mine)

Paul "felt" the pressure of his concern for the people. He felt that burden with a similar intensity that he felt the beatings and the sleeplessness.

Similarly, when we open the door to other people's pain, the awareness of that pain walks into our lives. The crisis is not our own. It is not part of our story in the same way that our own experiences are. But now we are aware of that pain, and it has an impact on us. So, we must figure out what to do with this awareness.

Reminding yourself of the following truths will help you to lead and encourage without becoming overwhelmed:

* This is someone else's story. Because it is someone else's story, I do not have the provision to carry it as they do. If I take this story as my own, I will add details and layers of pain that come from my own life perspective that may not be connected to the person but can affect my own life.

* If I take this story as my own, I will begin to "lead" rather than walk alongside.

* The only one who can handle the transfer of pain and suffering from another person is Jesus Christ. My job is to encourage the participant to place her pain and suffering on Him. Thus, my immediate reaction when the pain is placed in *my* "hands of awareness" should be to open my hands to Jesus and immediately leave it there.

Remembering these truths can help us to step back and experience the "awareness" of the pain without taking on the "burden" of that pain. It also helps us to move forward "in step" with the participant.

Another thing to consider when you feel burdened by a participant's story is that you might be impacted because of similar pain in your past. It might be that when you heard the participant share, your memories came flooding back, and some of those emotions might have risen to the surface. Some tears might even have flowed. That is okay. This response connects to the person telling the story. She will be able to tell that you "get it."

Of course, as leaders, we cannot become puddles on the floor. In a sense, we must hold ourselves together. So, if we are emotionally triggered in this way while someone is sharing, we can immediately seek God's help in keeping the connection with the participant rather than retreating into our own pain or taking over the story. God can help you do this.

Later, in private, you might need to spend time pouring and casting your emotions onto God. Your story is important. Your journey through pain and suffering toward healing is important. And we are all on this journey together. God will help you work through your own suffering as you take the hand of another who is in pain.

GRACE FOR LEADERS

We, as leaders, want to do our best—not for our personal glory, but for the group. But I will assure you now: you will not always do your best. You will not always say the right thing, show the best attention, interpret the speaker correctly. No one does. There will be times when you will leave the group and think, *Why did I say that?* Give yourself grace.

Most times when you make a misstep, you can simply move on and learn from the experience. But if it was serious, and there is something you need to say to a participant or to the group to rectify a situation, do so. It's okay to say, "I did not respond the way I wanted to. Let's think about this again."

You will not lead perfectly, but you can lead graciously. That includes accepting imperfection—in the participants and in yourself.

COURAGE AND PEACE FOR LEADERS

Do you feel God's call to come alongside those who are in pain? Are you ready?

The answer to the first question might be a resounding, "Yes! I hear and feel God asking me to become involved with others in this way." The answer to the second question, however, might be, "I am not sure!" If you don't quite feel ready for the task, know that it is normal and right to have some concern and hesitation. But remember that you will not be trying to help others in your own strength. You are dependent on the Good Shepherd, who is the only One who can bring true healing. Perhaps you can pour out your heart to Him in a prayer:

We hear Your voice calling us to listen to the pain of others.

Yet, we have our own pain.

We hear You telling us to offer our hands to others as they find their way.

Yet, there are times when our own footsteps are unsure.

We know that we are to offer the truth of Your words to others in their suffering.

Yet, sometimes in the dark, Your voice seems far away and we feel our own doubts.

Perhaps it is because of our own pain, our stumbling steps, and our uncertainties that we

can come alongside our brothers and sisters and tell them what we know to be true.

In our pain, we cry out to You and find You there, offering comfort.

When we stumble to find the way,

You shine light on the next step.

When we express our doubts,

You reassure us that You are God.

Help us now to offer ourselves, but only as a vessel that leads others to You.

Help us to offer reassuring words, but only as they are truth from You.

Help us to offer hope for the future, but only the sure hope of a future with You.

Prepare us, strengthen us, and protect us for our good, others' good, and Your glory.

Amen

Dear traveler,

Even though I don't know your story, I want you to know that I feel connected to you.

I am very much aware that our faithful Traveling Companion, our Creator, knows both of us, and so, in some way—maybe through this book or through our shared human experience of pain, or both—He is connecting us.

Like you, I am no stranger to suffering. In fact, I have been "living" this book for many years, often writing chapters "in the moment"—sometimes after a traumatic incident, other times upon gaining a newfound awareness of pain. During these times, my words would come: "Oh, God, I don't want to feel this, and I don't know what to do with it!" And I would hear His clear response: *"Write it down. There is another whom I love, who needs to hear this and know they are not alone."*

And now you are here: that *"another"* is you.

I am a visual person, and so I have sometimes pictured you holding this book in your hand, sitting with it in a quiet place, or setting it on the table beside your bed or chair. In the process, I have come to envision it as a companion for your journey—one that can lead you through the uncertainty, out of the numbness, and toward healing.

You alone will decide how closely to hold to this companion. You may be happy just to make its acquaintance—skimming through pages, picking up a thought or two—or you may find it a trusted friend with whom you can settle in for the long haul. But you might bear in mind just a few simple things as you make your decision.

First, know that the chapters are ordered to follow a continuous thought process, with each chapter building on previous ones; so, I recommend starting at the beginning and following it through.

Also, some chapters are longer and more intense than others, so don't be discouraged if you are in a chapter that feels like "too much." Moments of respite—visuals, short poems, or other light reading—are deliberately sprinkled into the mix, just when you might need encouragement. Many chapters also end with "A Bend in the Road," a short section that offers you time to be still and contemplate any new awareness or pending decision you may be facing. I encourage you not to pass over these sections—but don't force them either. If you aren't ready for a particular bend in the road, make a note, continue on, and circle back around later. Your strength and courage will grow slowly by slowly, and soon you will be able to return.

Finally, this book is not a project to complete and add to the shelf. There is no need to rush through to "the end." Your journey will be ever-unfolding, which means that even beyond the final pages of this book, your path may lead you back—to revisit a chapter, add to a bend in the road, or uncover a new layer.

So, you decide. *A New Song* will be here, in whatever capacity you need, as a companion on your journey through suffering.

I am here too. And our Traveling Companion, who knows us both, will never stop coming alongside.

Thoughtfully Yours,

Susan

INTRODUCTION TO THE GUIDE TEMPLATE

Any group book study requires planning if the group is to benefit not only from sharing together but also from the content of the book. Because *A New Song* has the potential to open many directions of conversation, it is particularly important to have a plan.

As a leader, you want the culture of your group to feel relaxed, unrushed, and welcoming, but you also want it to be directed and orderly. You can use the following guide as a framework to help you accomplish these goals within the twelve individual group sessions intended for this study.

HOW THE GUIDE IS ORGANIZED

Each chapter of this guide is devoted to one group session. The only exception is chapter 11, which features an exercise for participants to do in preparation for the final group meeting.

If you browse through the guide, you will probably notice that each session covers several consecutive chapters from the book. For example, Session 1 covers chapters 1–8 in *A New Song*. The sessions are developed to facilitate discussion around complementary themes that occur across those chapters.

In addition, each session in this guide has been presented in a specific format, or template, that will remain consistent throughout the study and provide you with a gentle, but stable, pathway for leading a group through discussion.

The layout of this standard template appears and is explained on the following pages.

A NEW SONG BOOK STUDY
SESSION NUMBER
CHAPTER NUMBERS COVERED
Name of 1st Chapter
Name of 2nd Chapter
Name of 3rd Chapter
And So On . . .

INTENTIONS: The direction in which we want to gently guide the participant for that session
The truth or principle that will be beneficial to healing
The tool or experience that can assist in moving forward with courage and peace

GREETING: This will be unique and personal to each group.

REFLECTION: A few sentences that remind participants of the basic themes and lessons discussed in the previous session.

OVERVIEW OF CHAPTERS FOR THIS SESSION: A summary of the main concepts covered in the chapters to be discussed this session. Ideally, participants will have completed the reading and activities in these chapters before group time.

INVITATION TO SHARE: Through pointed questions and discussion prompts, group members are encouraged to share the impressions and experiences they had while working through the chapters for this session. Questions and prompts are usually broken down by chapter and often relate to that section's bend(s) in the road.

PREFACE TO UPCOMING READING: A brief introduction to the reading assigned for the next session.

OPPORTUNITY FOR GROWTH: An opportunity to quickly draw attention to the bends in the road you will discuss at the next session.

COURAGE AND PEACE: An opportunity to bring the group to a close with calmness and confidence. Because our minds can become confused and muddled after discussing so many details related to our pain and where we should go next, this section will suggest words to use to recenter participants and encourage them to continue forward.

A KEY TO READING THE GUIDE

In the session template example, you may have noticed that while some text appeared inside a white box and some appeared inside a shaded box, most of it had no box around it at all. Here's a key to understanding what these different text formats indicate:

White boxes provide information meant only for the leader; for example, ideas on how to present certain materials or notes on how to approach participants when sharing about sensitive topics.

Shaded boxes highlight direct quotes from *A New Song* that relate to the discussion at hand. These excerpts may be read aloud and used freely within the group conversation.

Lined boxes are provided for leader notes:

All normal text—anything not within boxes—is suggested script for the leader. This script is what you will use to facilitate the bulk of the session.

HOW TO USE—AND NOT USE—THE SUGGESTED SCRIPT

Scripted text is not meant to define or constrict what you say. It is there to *help* you lead, to guide you in where to lead the conversation next. Do not read it aloud, word for word. Rather, use the thoughts that are given and make them your own.

Also feel free to add to the scripted material to make it more personal. You might say, for example, "This question was difficult for me" or "I appreciated this thought." The more you progress through the sessions, the more you will find your own expressive way to lead.

A good way to start preparing for a session is to read through the INTENTIONS segment, which is the text that appears inside the white box at the top of every session. This segment will provide you with a big-picture outline of the meeting, which you can keep in mind both at the beginning of each session and throughout, to ensure that the focus stays on track.

Use the GREETING segment as a prompt that guides you to start the meeting in a way that is meaningful to your particular members. For example, you may want to start by acknowledging a common event (the weather is always appropriate), a challenge in getting to the meeting, or something your group members have started to connect with in general day-to-day life.

The next segments—REFLECTION and OVERVIEW OF CHAPTERS FOR THIS SESSION—provide script that you can use to briefly summarize the previous session and introduce the current one.

Be aware that, in some sessions, the OVERVIEW OF CHAPTERS FOR THIS SESSION will be combined with the segment that normally follows it: INVITATION TO SHARE. Because their content is so closely related, however, having them combined should not impact the way you present the material to the group.

Once you are ready to initiate the INVITATION TO SHARE portion of the meeting, it might be helpful to reiterate one or two of the rules of etiquette (outlined in full in Session 1) as they apply to sharing. We all need these reminders from time to time, but they will become especially important as familiarity in the group grows.

As the leader, although you may share periodically in response to the discussion prompts in this section, it is not wise to share on every question. Also be mindful about keeping your sharing time brief—and without too many details. It is good for the group to get to know you and to feel your connection with them, however, so respond now and again when it is appropriate.

Also remember that the intention of this sharing time is to give participants the opportunity to express the heart of their stories in a *safe place*. The focus of the time is on the opportunity to *speak*—not on the opportunity to receive responses or advice. In fact, advice and quick, *assumed* connections from other participants (for example, "That's how it was for me" or "I was in a similar situation") are likely to discourage further sharing.

This is not to say that other participants cannot respond at all. It would be acceptable to express sympathy, for example. ("Mary, thank you for sharing that. I have felt a similar betrayal. I'm sorry it happened to you.") However, the primary "responder" to those who share should be you, the leader. Never allow a discussion where multiple participants begin to advise one another. You are the protector of the safe setting. You are the protector of the opportunity for these individuals to bring their pain into the light without the fear of comparison, shame, or the expectation to come to resolution.

Not every participant will respond to every question. It is not helpful to go around the circle, asking each person to share. This builds anxiety and becomes burdensome to everyone.

As more people in your group feel comfortable sharing, your time will go by quickly. So, watch your timing closely and move on to the next question, as needed, to protect your sharing time. Think ahead and be prepared to acknowledge the value of what was shared while encouraging more thought in the areas discussed—and then invite the group to move onward. Also, be prepared to find a way to bring the sharing to a close. This closing will not be a conclusion; there should be no insinuation that the participants are "done" with that conversation and cannot return to it. It is simply an acknowledgement that, due to the constraint of time, the group must move onto the next segment.

When you reach the PREFACE TO UPCOMING READING and OPPORTUNITY FOR GROWTH segments, avoid *teaching* the next chapters; simply provide a preview of what is to come. The purpose of these segments is to draw the participants into the reading by piquing their interest—not to spoon-feed it to them, in which case they might think they have heard enough to get by and skip doing the necessary work. You want the participants to read and work through the chapters themselves, winding their way through the nuances intuitively and with intention, because then they will engage with the material more personally—and that will make all the difference in their process of healing.

TIMING THE SESSION

Avoid "announcing" when you are ready to move onto the next segment. For example, don't say, "Now I am going to do the REFLECTION." Rather, transition smoothly from one part of your time to the next so that the gathering feels like a conversation with friends, not a regimented course.

It is also helpful to mentally note the time you spend on each segment. The goal is to move smoothly from one segment to the next without lingering too long in one place or rushing ahead too quickly. You can do this by noting on paper the estimated clock time at which you want to begin each segment. If you find that you get off-track in your timing by a minute or two in one segment, try to catch up in another area. Finding yourself sidetracked for even 5 or 10 minutes can make a difference in what you accomplish by the end of the session. Over time, the group will become accustomed to the expectations and appreciate your guidance.

A NEW SONG BOOK STUDY
SESSION 1

CHAPTERS 1–8

So Many Stories
An Invitation
". . . I Must Walk It Alone"
A New Path
A Different Kind of Journey
A Contemplative Journey
Etiquette For The Journey
Bends In The Road

NOTE: Session 1 will be unique from the other sessions because it introduces the book, its theme, and the author, and outlines the expectations for the group setting. There will be no REFLECTION or OVERVIEW OF CHAPTERS because participants will not be prepared to share, and some may not even have the book yet. In place of these portions, you will find the following discussion topics: INTRODUCTION, ETIQUETTE FOR THE JOURNEY, and EXPECTATIONS.

The overall intention of this first session, then, is for participants to come together on common ground.

Because participants will not have prepared, suggested excerpts from the book are noted in gray. Read these excerpts to the group or ask others to read them. (You might want to let the person know before the meeting so they can be prepared.) Encourage the rest of the group to open their books and follow along—and then encourage them to *re-read* the same portions later; they will absorb more when they can read privately, at their own speed.

If you lead a large group that divides into smaller groups for sharing time, be aware that you will not want to break out into these groups in Session 1 until you reach the INVITATION TO SHARE portion.

INTENTIONS: To present a clear introduction of this book study, including . . .
  - the acknowledgement of suffering and pain in our conversation,
  - the privilege of telling our stories as we seek healing,
  - the intention of the author to provide a safe way through pain and then forward, and
  - the intention of the group to compassionately take the journey together.

To describe this contemplative journey as different from others.

To give a brief introduction to the Opportunity For Growth for Session 2.

INTRODUCTION: The purpose of this book study is not so much to introduce something new; rather, it is to acknowledge something that is already in place and then discover how to respond to it in a healthy way.

From the time we were young, each of us had expectations for life—for events we would experience and relationships we would have. As we grew older, however, we were compelled to acknowledge that our expectations would not always be met.

Maturity taught us to accept, to adjust—and then to *move on.* Our survival demanded it; others demanded it; and the high-speed, never-pausing, constantly changing world around us demanded it. Even now, it seems that everything is constantly pulling (or pushing) us *forward.* Yet, there is something that seems stuck in place. Something that, try as we might, we cannot seem to move on from. That something is *suffering.*

Sometimes, we have difficulty acknowledging that we have truly experienced suffering. We minimize the experience with words like, "My suffering is not that bad compared to others," "I don't want to complain," "It's okay; it's over now," or "I don't have time to deal with it." But there is no scale of suffering by which we determine its merit for attention. Neither is there only one type of experience to which we can give the title of suffering; rather, painful experiences run the gamut, including disappointment, betrayal, abuse, grief, disillusionment, loss, abandonment, rejection, illness, and more. There is also no time limit on the effects of suffering.

Instead, our suffering is our suffering—and by that only, it merits attention. This is the reason for this study: *A New Song* provides the opportunity, and perhaps even the time, for us to acknowledge the suffering in our lives.

Susan Habegger, author of *A New Song*, gives us an invitation to this journey to acknowledge suffering. (Chapter 2: pages 5-6)

Susan also helps us understand this different kind of journey. (Chapter 5: pages 11-12)

Ultimately, we take this journey alone. But there is encouragement and accountability in companionship. So, when we do this book study as a group, we are deciding to take the journey alone *together*. This does not mean linking arms and pulling one another along at a single pace along one path. Each person's journey is one-of-a-kind. We travel at different speeds, encounter different obstacles, and respond in different ways. What it does mean is knowing that we are together on the path, each experiencing *similar*, yet *unique*, emotions and challenges. We can all glance around from our unique positions on the path and see familiar, compassionate faces.

ETIQUETTE FOR THE JOURNEY: Throughout this study, we will speak often of "conversations." These can be conversations the author has with you, conversations you have with yourself, conversations you have with each other, and perhaps, even conversations you have with God. These conversations are pivotal for healing, and our responses to them can powerfully influence the direction they will go.

For this reason, there is a code of behavior, or *etiquette*, that we must follow in a group setting. In general, this code of behavior comes from practicing the following attributes:

Respect. Patience. Compassion. Trust.

More specifically, we can apply these attributes to how we treat those who share personal stories and details in the group setting. A person's story is a valuable possession, and to share it with someone is an act of trust. In turn, the response to that act of trust can be crucial to that person's healing process. Most of us have had the experience of sharing part of our story with someone, only to be ridiculed, accused, or ignored. We know how that feels. Such negative responses can impose feelings of guilt and self-consciousness on the person who is sharing and reinforce their already looming lack of value, causing them to quickly close the door to their heart and to determine never to be so foolishly vulnerable again.

On the other hand, when we apply the etiquette of showing respect, patience, compassion, and trust to those who share personal information, we encourage sharing and promote healing by making the group an emotionally safe place for everyone.

Applying our code of conduct to sharing looks something like the following:
- Nothing we share will be repeated to others.
- Nothing we share will bring rejection, condemnation, or shame.
- Our sharing will not be met with advice on how we should fix the situation.
- We embrace the opportunity to share our stories while also giving attention to the time limitations and needs of others.

Another important thing to keep in mind: it is sometimes that very *quick expression of care* that can hinder the telling of the story. Our hearts often jump to give reassurance and answers to those who are sharing painful experiences, and although we may mean well, we can inadvertently devalue or minimize the suffering of someone else by being too quick to reassure. By giving quick answers, we enforce the expectation to "return to normal."

However, a kind smile, a nod of the head, a leaning in —these responses are *always welcome*.

We are *not* here to fix each other. We are not here to advise each other. We are here simply to be "together" on this journey. We are here to be compassionate witnesses to others' stories. Our job is not to pull someone forward but to walk alongside, to focus our attention on our own journeys while being a reassuring presence on the path we are all traveling together.

Finally, the etiquette that we show to each other during our group sessions is something that we should also extend to ourselves. The same kind of consideration that we give each other does not always come as naturally when listening and speaking to ourselves, so we might need to stop often on our journey to think about this as well.

Susan encourages us to be good companions to ourselves:

(Excerpt from Chapter 7: pages 17-20) Just as you would get to know others in a group through their sharing, you will get to know yourself. There will be times that you like what you see; you will "recognize" and feel comfortable with that person. There will be other times when you are surprised, even shocked, by what is expressed or felt, even when it is in your own words or in your own heart. When that happens, how will you respond?

Respect. Patience. Compassion. Trust. Truth.

Let's begin with *respect*. At all times, *show respect for yourself*. Treat yourself with the same honor that you would extend to another who was sharing their story. An honest "story-telling" is ragged and often, uninviting. Yet, we show respect to the storyteller by being attentive. In the same way, no matter what comes, listen carefully to yourself. Don't turn away when the picture isn't pretty.

Show respect also by shutting out distractions. As you would for another, set aside time for yourself that is protected. Give time and full attention to yourself. You and your story are valuable.

Next, be *patient*. It is likely that your pain has been growing for months or even years, so it will not be resolved overnight. Do not start your journey by drawing a finish line. Allow yourself to take a slow pace, rather than measuring success by your progress. Don't be discouraged when an emotion that you thought you had conquered sweeps over you unexpectedly. Don't feel guilty when you must retrace some of your steps. Don't give into defeat when, in that process of retracing, you discover more layers of pain. Instead, it is necessary to wait quietly for yourself.

Have *compassion*. Think carefully about the words that you say to yourself. Are they kind? Are they accusatory? Are they echoes of what you have heard others say to you? Is it always necessary to speak? Are you able to compassionately listen to yourself without an immediate reactionary response or call to action?

Now, *trust* yourself enough to be honest. As you consider your own role in your story, you might feel the temptation to hide, to deny the rawness of what comes to the surface. I encourage you not to give into this temptation. Do not pretend or play a part. The journey will be wasted if you base your next steps on what you could have or should have done, rather than on what really occurred. There will be no real healing if you put on a face that you think will be more pleasing to others or even to yourself. There will be no resolution if you craft responses as if you were scripting a play.

Finally, commit to *truth*. Sometimes the truth will bring an immediate sense of freedom. Sometimes it will sting. But always, truth will move you in the right direction. Truth—real truth— even with its jagged edges, will always move you further from captivity and closer to healing.

Most of us assume that we know ourselves. And many of us may. However, we always get to know someone more intimately when we go on a journey with them. By being your own companion on this journey, you will get to know yourself more. As you do, you will begin to discover what healing looks like and feels like for *you*. Your path of suffering is not the same as anyone else's; and your new song will not have the same melody as another's. So, you should never expect to fit your expression of healing into a preconceived checklist of accomplishments.

In the midst of it all, the intention is for you to feel safe, to be heard, and to become aware that you are *seen, known, and loved*.

Be a good companion to yourself. And if the path ever seems desolate for a moment, know that you are never completely alone.

BENDS IN THE ROAD: Journeys are often hurried. We want to arrive at our destination as quickly as possible! But this one is different.

Susan introduces a descriptive of this "unhurried" journey:

(Excerpt from Chapter 6: pages 13-15) The journey through suffering toward healing is not a journey of quick steps, comparative progress, or rushed restoration. Thinking about it as *contemplative* can help us to slow down, give us direction, and remind us to breathe.

Think of contemplative time as an opportunity to "clear away the clutter" with purpose. Some people like to be organized. They clear away clutter because they like the look and feel of orderliness. They are happy with unused empty space because it allows them the freedom to use that space however they need, whenever they need—to complete a project, for example.

Likewise, we must *clear some clutter* so that we have the space to think and move and do what we need to do more freely. Things such as . . . undistracted thinking, unhurried pondering, attentive reflection.

The very idea of clearing away all distraction might feel threatening. Televisions, radios, phones, computers, and books provide endless interminable background noise to "protect" us from such attentive reflection.

Virtually every fragment of our daily routines compels us toward activity and response. Every task and every opportunity for input persuades us of its immediate importance to our well-being and our productivity.

It might also be that well-intentioned people have tried to help you in your suffering by attempting to provide in some way—with a new job, a new relationship, or financial stability—something to turn the old to new, the bad to good. Such provision can be helpful; there are legitimate needs to be met. Yet, the underlying message is still the rushed expectation to *return to normalcy*.

Again, this response to suffering presses it down out of sight; but it does not disappear. It only puts on a mask until a moment when it resurfaces unexpectedly and perhaps with more intensity. Our own quick responses and others' expectations oblige us to move quickly forward.

Perhaps, one of the most precious gifts you can receive in suffering is a quiet and safe place for the journey. No expectations, except truth—and even that may come in layers. No promises, except that your story will be heard.

Undistracted thinking. Unhurried pondering. Attentive reflection. One would almost think you are in no hurry to get to the destination. And there is the treasure. *The value of the journey is the journey itself.* This *contemplative journey* is a gift to you.

A journey for the purpose of spending time to consider our emotions and thoughts might sound inviting, but we often find it difficult to schedule "unhurried time." For this reason, at various points throughout the book, Susan will advise that we are coming to "a bend in the road." Each bend in the road usually includes a journaling activity that you can do directly in the pages of the book. This offers you a time to *slow down* and contemplate, to focus on a particular challenge of the journey. It is these bends in the road that will bring more clarity.

Be aware that, although the bends in the road may include activities, these are not to be viewed as assignments. Instead, they are opportunities for growth. Some bends will be more difficult than others to process though, and some might seem unnecessary at first, until you start the work. But when approached with an open heart, most (if not all) of them will lead to discoveries and awareness that help "clear away the clutter," so that you can move more freely toward healing.

EXPECTATIONS:

We will follow a general template for our time together, so that you will know what to expect out of each meeting. There will be a short introduction to the concepts in the chapters we will be discussing. These are the chapters we will have read and considered before group time and will share about today.

Then there will be an opportunity to express your responses to the bends in the road from the reading. Please note that you will never be required to share with the group. The most important thing you can do during this time is to ponder the truths and awareness that come as you consider your steps on the journey. You will know when the time is right to share a particular part of that journey. We will end with a brief introduction to the upcoming lesson.

What is expected of you, as the participant?

- You are encouraged to attend every session. You are not required to complete that session's reading or journaling activities in order to attend; however, you will receive from this journey in proportion to the effort and time you give to it. In addition, safety and trust within the group will grow through the consistency of our attendance and sharing.

- When sharing parts of your story, be careful about sharing details of others that you might regret later.

- Do not respond to others' sharing by giving advice, comparing their story to yours, or critiquing their ideas.

- Hold in confidence the stories represented in this room. Do not talk about them even with other participants. This is a gift we give to each other—the same gift others are giving to you.

NOTE: This is a good time to share details specific to your group meetings, such as the location, day of the week, and start and end times.

INVITATION TO SHARE: Now that we have spent some time together and know a bit more about how we will spend our time in coming weeks, maybe some of you are open to sharing briefly why you are interested in this book study or this topic. Maybe you want to share why this is a difficult—or easy—decision for you. We will share only briefly tonight, knowing that we will have many more opportunities in future sessions.

PREFACE TO UPCOMING READING: During our session today, we read excerpts from Chapters 1–8. You might want to reread the complete chapters and make notes in your book. In future sessions, you will read particular chapters in preparation for our group sharing. We will not generally read the chapters during group time. Our next session will consider Chapters 9–14.

We want to express our story. We want it to be heard, even if only by us. We are ready to start the journey. But how do we begin? If we are asked to tell about our lives, we often begin with a list of experiences. One after another. There are "ups" and "downs." The reality is that your story is more than just individual events. There is a tapestry that weaves through and around and between each experience. Life is a story. Sometimes, the between-the-event times are just as descriptive of that narrative. These are the moments of response and adjustment to the change, the pain, the unexpected, and uninvited.

The upcoming reading will help us begin the journey. Be prepared that we are not going to discover solutions or quick fixes as we take the initial steps. We are going to look closely at suffering and identify our natural response to it. We will also be reminded that our stories are so much more than random events, mistakes, or unjust actions of others. Our stories are full of value, purpose, and beauty.

OPPORTUNITY FOR GROWTH: Your first bend in the road will come immediately after the chapter "How Do We Begin?" (Chapter 9). You will read about the ups and downs and positives and negatives of life, and then you will have opportunity to put pieces of your life on paper. Follow the gentle guidance provided without rushing ahead. Avoid trying to accomplish this all in one sitting. Spend some time and then revisit it. The picture comes clear with time and unhurried pondering.

COURAGE AND PEACE:

Read the note from Susan: Dear traveler (Pages xxi-xxii)

CLOSING

A NEW SONG BOOK STUDY
SESSION 2

CHAPTERS 9–14

How Do We Begin?
Your Story
Cue Entrance: Suffering
A Deep Breath
Survival—Our Common Response To Suffering
Beginning To Focus

INTENTIONS: To help build a foundation for our stories
To identify events: positive and negative events, highs and lows
To enlarge our vision to more than just one moment in time
To name suffering
To acknowledge our common response to suffering
To begin to focus on one predominant awareness of pain that needs attention
To give a brief introduction to the Opportunity For Growth in Session 3

GREETING: This will be unique and personal to each group.

REFLECTION: In our last session, we opened up the conversation on suffering. Perhaps, you weren't sure that this topic or this book study was something you actually wanted to do. Perhaps, you are still wavering. If so, I would like to encourage you with the reminder that we are taking this journey together.

Also, now that you have begun to read and "interact" with the book, you have probably encountered the reality of this contemplative journey. Hopefully, you were a good companion to yourself so that you felt safe and heard.

OVERVIEW OF CHAPTERS FOR THIS CHAPTER and INVITATION TO SHARE: Life with its series of events can be an overwhelming image—too much to take in all at once and certainly too much to express. So, our first bend in the road provided us with the opportunity to sort out some of these events, into happy and sad, positive and negative, highs and lows. The second bend in the road then encouraged us to begin to narrow our focus to one source of pain.

It prompted us to listen for the part of our story crying out for attention. This is our opportunity to share with each other some of what we discovered during these bends in the road.

First, though, let's remember that our time of sharing is to be safe. We will repeat nothing outside this space. We do not need to package up what we share as a presentation or bring it to a positive conclusion. We are not going to respond to each other with advice. We are here to add companionship on this journey of healing, however that looks for you.

1. (Chapter 9) This might be the first time some of you have created a timeline of events in your life. What was this experience like for you? What did you observe as you looked at the highs and lows? Did you see any trends? Was there anything that surprised you?

2. (Chapter 10) Let's take some time with the chapter called "Your Story." (Read it aloud.) What statement spoke to you about your own story? Why, or in what way?

3. (Chapter 13) In Chapter 13, we read that our common response to suffering is to hide it or package it, or to attempt to put life back together the way it was or the way we thought it was. Did you see yourself in this description? How has trying to reach a resolution "too quickly" prevented healing for you in some situation?

4. (Chapter 14) The next bend in the road came as we began to focus in on our storyline. Because we often have numerous moments of pain in our lives, we discovered that we cannot come face to face with every one of them. Was it difficult for you to focus in on one source of pain? If so, consider whether finding your focal point might involve tracing back several events to a common source or a common emotion. Or perhaps, this narrowing of focus landed on something different than you anticipated. What surprised you about this process? What was painful about it? How did determining a focus help you?

PREFACE TO UPCOMING READING: Our next session will consider Chapters 15–21.

Suffering, or the awareness of suffering, is a before/after moment. This reality comes alive in our next reading. Resolution is good. Coming to peace is good. But what is it that we come to peace "with?"

Susan invites us to become familiar with suffering:

> Of all that we could wish to become "familiar with," suffering likely is not at the top of our list. Yet, once suffering connects with us personally, it is wise to respond in kind—because when we avoid it or deny its presence in our lives, its effects only grow stronger.
>
> In other words, now that we have been properly introduced to suffering, it is time to move forward in the relationship. It is time to really *see* the suffering that has entered your story—to acknowledge its presence as something more than an event on a timeline; to recognize it as something real and personal. (Chapter 18 Page 55)

We will also encounter a word that often comes into conversations around pain: *trauma*. The term *trauma* is usually one that we either embrace too willingly or immediately run from. By guiding us through a conversation about the term, Susan enables us to respond to it with discernment and courage rather than fear.

OPPORTUNITY FOR GROWTH: In our reading for the next session, our first opportunity for contemplation will be at a bend in the road that encourages us to identify a few of the differences between how life was (or how we thought it was) and how life is now—after our awareness of our particular pain (Chapter 15).

You likely have never considered that an ID card for trauma would be helpful, and yet it is. Because trauma's tactics often attack unexpectedly, we can only begin to take back control and move forward in healing when we become familiar enough with the identity of trauma to recognize it and call it to accountability (Chapter 18).

As our conversations stir up emotions and responses related to events, people, sources of pain, unspoken anxiety, and more, finding words to describe how we feel can seem difficult or even impossible. This is why the next bend in the road—"How Do You Feel?" (Chapter 19)—provides images to help us express the emotions of our stories. This exercise may touch us in unexpected ways.

COURAGE AND PEACE:

Every event, spoken or unspoken, is significant.
Every moment, positive or negative, is important.
This life, your life, is valuable.

This relationship with suffering will not overwhelm you. You will not be consumed. Suffering is part of your journey, but it is not your identity.

Each bend in the road holds opportunity . . .
for courage and for peace.

CLOSING

A NEW SONG BOOK STUDY
SESSION 3

CHAPTERS 15–21

Life as It Was; Life As It Is Now
Beauty Is
Perspective Shift
Becoming Familiar With Suffering
How Do You Feel?
My Traveling Companion
I Am Not Consumed

INTENTIONS: To help identify how life is changed by a painful event or by the awareness of pain

To come to peace with *the way life is now*

To lessen the threat of trauma by becoming familiar with its negative effects

To express an emotional connection to suffering

To understand that suffering and trauma will not consume

To give a brief introduction to the Opportunity For Growth in Session 4

GREETING: This will be unique and personal to each group.

REFLECTION: Our stories are beginning to come to life. We understand that there is no way to care for the extended pain without first giving attention to the original wound. This can be difficult, however, and we will experience varied emotions in the process. So, we must encourage each other not to put our pain back in the box and turn the key. We must encourage each other, instead, to keep moving forward with courage and peace.

OVERVIEW OF CHAPTERS FOR THIS SESSION and INVITATION TO SHARE: Our reading for this session helped us clarify some important truth about our relationship with suffering. We use enormous amounts of strength and resources when we attempt to put life back together the way it was—or the way we thought it was—before the crisis; we also cause more pain for ourselves, because we are attempting an impossible task. True internal peace can only begin to surface as we accept and reconcile with the way life is now.

1. (Chapter 15) The first bend in the road invited us to more clearly define the *before* and the *after*. This takes some intentional effort. What are some of the differences you discovered in your life as you considered what was and what is now? What have you been resisting about these changes? What "rearrangements" in your life need attention and acceptance?

2. (Chapter 18) Susan encourages us to become familiar with the characteristics of trauma. This understanding will help us recognize the red flags in our lives so that we can protect ourselves. As such, our familiarity with the negative effects of suffering will not make us weak; instead, it will instill courage. Which of the characteristics mentioned in this chapter did you recognize in your own life? Which characteristics have you experienced recently?

3. (Chapter 19) "How do you feel?" is a question that is difficult to answer. The images in our second bend in the road may have opened the door to our ability to express emotion as we attempted to respond to this question. Perhaps, you had no words to share but could simply point to the image and say, "This." Or maybe an image opened the door for you to further tell your story. Let's share our experiences with these images, remembering that our purpose is to be compassionate witnesses.

4. (If time—Chapter 17) Susan reminds us that we are seeing things from a new perspective. Some of these perspectives include the following:

   - The undeniable awareness of suffering
   - The inbuilt desire for resolution or peace
   - The realization that there is potential for repeated pain

   If you look closely, do you sense any of these perspectives troubling your own decision-making and reasoning?

PREFACE TO UPCOMING READING: In this session, and in the reading that led up to it, we spent time looking back for the purpose of giving needed attention to the pain; looking back, we learned, is a necessary part of turning forward. We also learned much about ourselves and our responses to suffering as we paid attention to our expression of pain.

As we continue forward, reading Chapters 22–27, which we will discuss at our next session, we will begin to deal with this pain by speaking truth into it.

In Susan's words: We are becoming ever more familiar with the suffering that has touched our lives. We have opened our eyes to its traumatic effects that want to consume. We know that trauma, if left to its own devices, will envelop every part of our being—body, mind, and soul. Yet, we have been open to giving suffering its day. We have looked; we have felt; we have engaged. We have also been given the opportunity to step away from that initial all-consuming control with which pain first grasped us. The next step in our journey will be to speak truth into the reality of our suffering. (Chapter 27 page 93)

OPPORTUNITY FOR GROWTH: In our upcoming conversations, both in the book and in the next session, we will begin to move in closer to our experience of suffering. If you are not sure this is something you want to do, keep in mind that the next bend in the road will be one of the most expressive you have had; it may be just what you need. Have your colored pencils ready. (Chapter 22)

Susan will also speak about the reality of our responses to pain, including the words we say to ourselves and the thoughts we think. Sometimes our response is a silent resignation within our spirits that implies this is what we deserve—what we should expect. This kind of self-talk needs some attention. (Chapter 25)

COURAGE & PEACE: As you travel this journey of healing, sometimes feeling strong—and sometimes feeling undone, be reminded of these truths:

You are a unique and intentional creation by The Perfect Creator.
You are declared valuable by The Perfect Creator.
You are seen. You are known. You are loved.

CLOSING

A NEW SONG BOOK STUDY
SESSION 4

CHAPTERS 22–27

A Picture
Look Away
To Be Fully Known
This Is Just My Life
Your Path
A Beginning And An End

INTENTIONS: To help participants express their stories through color and image on the page

To clarify the balance between contentment and unsettlednesss

To consider the truth that peace and justice can coexist

To understand that the imminent threat of suffering has a beginning and an end

To give a brief introduction to the Opportunity For Growth in Session 5

GREETING: This will be unique and personal to each group.

REFLECTION: In our last session, we discovered some ways to protect ourselves. We looked at how the reality of life before and life after needs to affect our expectations so that we can avoid repeated hurt. We also added a layer of protection for ourselves by becoming familiar with the characteristics of trauma, knowing the more familiar we become with suffering, the more we will replace fear with strength.

OVERVIEW OF CHAPTERS FOR THIS SESSION and INVITATION TO SHARE: With each session, we are introduced to a new way to look at suffering. The reading for this session gave us the opportunity to add a new dimension to suffering through artistic expression. It also showed us that we have the freedom to "look away" when we need a break from engaging with our pain. We were further encouraged to find that one of our deepest longings—*to be known*—is a truth we can hold onto and to discover that the events of our suffering have beginnings and endings.

1. (Chapter 22) Whether you consider yourself an artist or not, you were invited to express your suffering with color and shape and image on the page. This exercise was meant only for you, so we will not share our pictures, but would anyone like to share how this exercise felt? Did you surprise yourself with your creation?

2. (Chapter 25) "This is just my life." Maybe you have never said this aloud; maybe you have just resigned yourself to the idea that you are to accept, without question, the pain that someone else inflicts on you. How do we balance mercy and justice? How do we show contentment and still give heed to the unsettledness? Have you experienced this dilemma in your life? What did you learn that will help you?

3. (Chapter 27) One of the negative effects of suffering is that it wants to consume us and hold us in fear. An event that happened years ago still threatens us now. We created a timeline of our suffering to discover when the event started and then when the imminent threat ended. This was difficult, but it helped us to set boundaries for those times when past suffering threatens our current sense of well-being. For those of us whose suffering is ongoing, we learned that it is helpful to discover "smaller" beginnings and endings within the continuing experience. Let's talk about the bend in the road here. What truth did you pinpoint? How can this new awareness help you set some boundaries on the fear that pushes into your everyday life?

4. (If time—Chapter 24) Many of us have the desire to *be known*. We sometimes even wish that someone would do something for us "just because they know me so well." But the reality is that, often, we are not known as we would like to be. Alternatively, many of us wonder, *If people really knew me, would they still like me? Would they still love me?* This is why one of the most fulfilling parts of our relationship with God is to understand that we are fully known and yet fully loved by Him. He sees you. He knows you. He loves you. So, what do you want God to see in you? What do you want God to know about you? What part of the "real you" needs some attention?

PREFACE TO UPCOMING READING: Our next session will consider Chapters 28 - 32.

We will discuss how, although our pain is familiar to us and we know what it feels like, we are not always sure of its source. We will also talk about how, although the details of every story are different—the suffering is personal and the trauma that follows is unique—there are some common seeds that trauma sows in each of us. This discovery will help us in practical ways as we move toward healing.

OPPORTUNITY FOR GROWTH: It might be fairly obvious to us by now that things have changed. But what may not be so obvious is what we have lost. Because of our crisis, our suffering, something is gone. *Many* things are gone. And the list of those things often goes beyond the obvious.

We must stop to think carefully about the tangible and intangible losses we have experienced, because they can cause grief that affect us physically, mentally, and spiritually. One of the upcoming bends in the road will help us do just that. This bend includes several layers, however, and we will not embrace them all at once. Rather, we will take small, but intentional, steps in a particular order. So, please do not jump ahead. Be a patient and compassionate traveling companion for yourself.

By the time we get through Chapters 28–32, we will have done the following:

- – Acknowledge loss
- – Identify the loss
- – Look honestly at the emotions that come from loss
- – Respond to the loss without attempting to replace it
- – Mourn the loss

COURAGE & PEACE: You may be doing something that you have never done before—intentionally getting to know suffering and pain, and particularly *your* pain. As you go through this process, you might feel at times like you are getting weaker, even coming undone.

But the truth is that you are gaining strength. You are gaining courage. You are acquiring truths that will help you move forward in healing. So, stay on the journey.

We are not all in the same place, but we can see each other. We know we are not alone.

CLOSING

A NEW SONG BOOK STUDY
SESSION 5

✦

CHAPTERS 28–32

Discovering Loss
Emotions: A Tangled Mess
Mourning Loss
Casting
What Is Left Of Me?

INTENTIONS: To help identify the losses from suffering—the obvious and the hidden

To uncover the many emotions of loss

To intentionally plan to mourn the loss

To understand and embrace the idea of "casting" cares on God

To experience the release of the burden of loss

To be assured that, despite all that is lost, substance is protected and can never be lost

To give a brief introduction to the Opportunity For Growth in Session 6

GREETING: This will be unique and personal to each group.

REFLECTION: You may have noticed that we continue to build on our familiarity with suffering. We have done this through words, through images, and through our own expression of color and visual on paper. Last week we created a timeline of suffering. All of these experiences help us bring our suffering into the light. We are recognizing the harmful effects that can linger. Why are we spending this time? We are actually becoming more aware, which makes us stronger and frees us from the manipulation of the pain.

OVERVIEW OF CHAPTERS FOR THIS SESSION and INVITATION TO SHARE: The readings this week were quite intense. Our desire is to walk towards healing. Yet here we are digging deep to discover loss and pain. As Susan says:

Loss *IS*. Loss demands attention in some way. If we are to move toward healing, we must identify it and give it the attention it desperately longs for.

Doing so is not an accusation of or attack on your well-being. Rather, it is a loving conversation with yourself to say, "What are you missing? What was taken from you without your permission? Let's acknowledge what is gone." It is a gift of love and nurturing to yourself to acknowledge and talk about something that is causing pain. (Chapter 28 page 102)

Together, let's acknowledge what is gone and how we will respond.

1. (Chapter 28) Minimizing loss. Attempting to replace loss as quickly as possible. Which of these common responses to loss resonates with you?

2. (Chapter 28) This bend in the road took some contemplation. There may be quick answers and then layers of loss that need time and effort to uncover. The following are the questions posed to us.

What was once here that is now gone?
What has been taken from me that I did not willingly give?
What empty places do I see . . . or sense . . . or feel?
What do I reach out to grasp, only to find that it is no longer there?
What might have been possible, but no longer is?

Some of you might want to share a particular loss. Some of you might want to describe what this experience was like for you. Were you able to pinpoint losses that you had not acknowledged previously? Let's share, remembering that this is a safe place where your story is held in confidence. We will not advise you—we will be a witness to the loss.

3. (Chapter 29) It was inevitable that we would feel emotion during this part of the journey—and at many other times. We have the opportunity to acknowledge even those emotions that might have surprised us or those we were trying to deflect or resist. What emotions were you able to acknowledge? Were there any that you added to the list?

4. (Chapter 30) Acknowledging loss is the first step. However, if we carry that burden we will be weighed down. "Feeling" the loss is not the same as "mourning" for it. To mourn is to intentionally give attention and value to the loss. Maybe we thought that was good for the loss of someone through death, but not relevant for other kinds of loss. Susan reminds us that every loss needs attention. Was this a new thought for you? Was it helpful? Have you taken any action towards this process of mourning?

5. (Chapter 31) We uncovered the loss. We felt the emotion of it. We have entered the mourning process. This is painful and can feel very heavy. Our perfect traveling companion knows this and is waiting to help relieve the burden. God invites us to cast this burden on Him and embrace the promise that He is able to absorb our grief. What plans do you have for "casting?" What does this invitation mean to you?

PREFACE TO UPCOMING READING: Our next session will consider Chapters 33–40.

We are coming to a place in our journey where "coming to peace" might sound like a good thing. One of the first chapters you read this week touches on a personal note before moving on. Susan shares her feelings of self-accusation. We consider how we can respond in a healthy way when those thoughts attempt to keep our focus in the past. And then comes the invitation to intentionally and bravely turn our focus in a new direction.

OPPORTUNITY FOR GROWTH: I must alert you that there are multiple bends in the road for our next session. The first helps us talk to ourselves about self-accusation. (Chapter 34) The second gives us opportunity to talk to the suffering. (Yes, we now are familiar enough with suffering to have a conversation with it—and maybe even set some boundaries on it.) (Chapter 35)

We will also have some honest conversations about our "comfortableness" with our pain. (Chapter 36–38) And finally, we will begin to see beyond and around and through the suffering. (Chapters 39–40)

COURAGE & PEACE: You have been working very hard. The emotional and even physical strength needed for this journey is undeniable. We are here to give courage to each other.

In you, the brokenhearted . . . is beauty. In you, who mourn . . . is beauty.
As you journey through suffering . . . you are not destroyed, but purified.
Your story has purpose.
Your pain has value.
You are a planting of the Lord who displays the splendor of the Living God.

(Chapter 33 page 131)

CLOSING

A NEW SONG BOOK STUDY
SESSION 6

CHAPTERS 33–40

Where Is Beauty?
A New Villain
Resolution
A Strange Comfortableness
A New Pair Of Shoes
Moving Forward
Vision Therapy
Where Am I Headed?

INTENTIONS: To safely express self-accusations and receive assurance

To speak courageously to suffering, setting a boundary against full-scale intrusion

To honestly identify ways that we may be comfortable in our pain

To adjust focus to find the good without denying the pain

To begin to think beyond the next hours of survival;
to engage in life with expectation

To give a brief introduction to the Opportunity For Growth in Session 7

GREETING: This will be unique and personal to each group.

REFLECTION: We are all familiar with the idea of mourning the loss of loved ones; such feelings of loss are expected. In our last session, we talked about the importance of identifying and mourning other types of loss in our lives. This was an important step forward on our journey. We reminded ourselves that even in all the loss, we are not consumed. God is able to absorb our grief and protect the substance of who we are, and because of this truth, we can continue to move forward.

OVERVIEW OF CHAPTERS FOR THIS SESSION and INVITATION TO SHARE: We started this section of reading with a look at self-accusation and the road to resolution. And then the journey toward peace really began. Perhaps, we were surprised to hear that we can become somewhat comfortable in our pain—that we might need nudging to endure the uncomfortableness of new shoes and persuasion to open our eyes to the good in our lives, without denying the reality of the pain. But where are we actually headed through all of this? Let's talk about it.

1. In Chapter 34, Susan reminds us: There will likely come a time (or maybe it already has come) when —whether with some validity or with no justification at all—you accuse yourself for some part of your suffering.

   Did you connect with this suggestion? Were you disturbed by it? How did you respond to this idea emotionally? Was it helpful to acknowledge this and come to peace with it?

2. (Chapter 35) We have come to a place where "we accept the reality of the pain and suffering that happened to us but refuse to live under its control." What concessions have you made and what boundaries have you set with your suffering?

3. (Chapter 36–38) Susan is honest with us, which helps us to be honest with ourselves. How have the pain and suffering become comfortable to you? In what ways does this new forward journey feel a bit uncomfortable? What has convinced you to fear or avoid moving forward?

4. (Chapter 39) We are reminded that we are not trying to create a story of good to offset the pain in our lives; rather, we are attempting to give ourselves the freedom and encouragement to see the good that is there. The painful event never disappears, but it can be put in its proper place to allow what is positive and good to also have its rightful place. Let's talk about this experience of vision therapy. Was it difficult? What *good* are you beginning to see in, around, and beyond your suffering?

5. (If time—Chapter 40) According to this chapter, "Healing is now bringing some changes to life. Simple actions that once seemed overwhelming begin to make sense." What is starting to shift or change for you? What hints do you see that you are moving toward healing rather than staying hunkered down in survival?

PREFACE TO UPCOMING READING: Our next session will consider Chapters 41-49.

For some of you, our next reading will be familiar. For others, it might open a conversation that you have never heard or that you have avoided. Even for those who claim to deny God, He usually comes up in a conversation about suffering. If there is a God . . .

Why? floats into our conversation, longing for an answer and yet without expectation of one that could satisfy. In the moment of the query, we can imagine no *why* that could justify the incomprehensible suffering. We will not come to resolution with the question "Why is there suffering?" but we will discover principles to help us come to peace with the idea of suffering. We will look at four questions to help us along this part of the journey:

- Why is there suffering in the world?
- Why did suffering happen to me?
- Where is God in the suffering?
- Why did God allow this to happen?

OPPORTUNITY FOR GROWTH: The only way this conversation will be helpful and bring resolution is if we are honest. This is the reason we will begin with the opportunity to voice our *whys*. (Chapter 41)

We will consider the ways that we see evidence of a broken world around us. (Chapter 43)

We will express how we have personally experienced the world's brokenness. (Chapter 44)

In all of the brokenness, is there *good*? Is God good? Why doesn't it *feel* good? (Chapter 46)

We will welcome Naomi back into the story and see what we might learn from her response to suffering—and to God. (Chapter 48)

In the midst of it all, Where *is* God? (Chapter 49)

This segment of chapters calls for quiet time and thought, not just once but over a period of days.

COURAGE AND PEACE: Approach the coming days with the confidence that grows from knowing yourself more fully and from being held close and protected by your good and perfect Traveling Companion. Your vision is clarifying and your heart is becoming more steady. Take deep breaths, as needed, and feel the strength that is building within. Individually—and together—we are moving in a good direction.

CLOSING

A NEW SONG BOOK STUDY
SESSION 7

※～∽

CHAPTERS 41–49

Voicing The Question
Four Common Whys
Why Is There Suffering?
Why Did Suffering Happen To Me?
Where Is God In The Suffering?
Why Did God Allow This To Happen?
A Visual Of Suffering
Remembering Naomi
Where Is God In The Storm?

INTENTIONS: To open up the conversation of "Why?"

> To engage in the conversation of what to do with God in suffering and pain
>
> To express and comprehend the realities of suffering and protection as related to God
>
> To embrace the comfort and assurance of "God With Us in the storm
>
> To give a brief introduction to the Opportunity For Growth in Session 8

GREETING: This will be unique and personal to each group.

REFLECTION: In subtle and intentional ways, we are beginning to turn our focus from looking back to looking forward. We acknowledged the familiarity we have with suffering and determined to put on a new pair of shoes. Perhaps, getting forward is taking more effort that we thought it would. It is sometimes difficult to release the negative and to begin to embrace what's positive and good in our story. But we have determined that we want to live with awareness of both our suffering *and* our blessings. Both are part of our story, and both are valuable.

OVERVIEW OF CHAPTERS FOR THIS SESSION: Susan opened Chapter 41 by summarizing our journey up to this point; she reminded us that we have taken time, we have worked, we have gained strength and discovered peace along the way. Then she guided us to slow down to consider a question that is no doubt intertwined in many of our thoughts: "Why?"

"Why is there suffering?" is the first question we explored, and to do so, we returned to the beginning. We remembered God's perfect creation—His good creation. We remembered Adam and

Eve's disobedience and the suffering that entered God's good world. And we realized that because of that one event, the world is now broken; and because the world is broken, there is suffering.

We then discussed the question "Why did suffering happen to me?" Because the world is broken, suffering is all around us. We cannot live perfectly to avoid it, and so, we are touched by suffering simply because we live in this world. We experience suffering because it is part of the road we must travel here on earth.

"Where is God in my suffering?" Perhaps this was the hardest question. God tells us about Himself: He is all-knowing, all-present, and all-powerful. God is not ignorant, unaware, or distracted; neither is He far off or powerless. Therefore, God was with you during your event of suffering, God is with you today, and God will be with you in the future. There is no suffering where God is not present. With God, there is no suffering that can destroy us. With Him, there is always the potential for healing.

INVITATION TO SHARE: What do we do with God in the story of our pain? How do we explain the events that enter our lives? The topic of our readings this past week may be familiar to you. Or maybe you have not considered this problem or have avoided it. Whatever the case, the best way for us to heal and come to peace is to open up these conversations so that we can come to some logical and truthful conclusions. We are not looking for answers to explain our pain away. Rather, we are seeking truth that keeps us from being swept away in despair or bitterness.

1. (Chapter 41) Even if we do not ask the *why* questions aloud, they weave in and out of our responses to the events in our lives. This bend in the road invited us to voice the *why* questions that we may have held in check until now. Would anyone like to share a *why*—with assurance that there will be no judgement, rebuke, or shame?

2. (Chapter 43) There is suffering because this world is broken. We don't have to look far to see this truth revealed around us: "We experience suffering because it is part of the road we must travel." How did you mentally respond when you read that statement? Had you previously been holding some hope that you would be able to avoid suffering if you just did x, y, or z?

3. (Chapter 44) And now it begins to get personal. Perhaps, we tried to protect ourselves, but the muddy water splashed on us, so now we carry the evidence that the broken world has touched us. What can you share that expresses *your* experience of the world's brokenness?

4. (Chapters 45, 47–49) The idea of God being with us in suffering is difficult for some people. However, the idea of suffering *without* God is also frightening. Have you had any experience of gaining peace by opening your heart and mind to the presence of God with you in suffering?

5. (If time—Chapter 46) God is good. All that God does is good. This is sometimes a hard truth, and yet, it is a pivotal point in our journey. How do we respond to the idea of *good* when it doesn't look or feel good? How could it impact our daily response to pain if we could actually trust that someone with the power to back it up truly wants only good for us?

PREFACE TO UPCOMING READING: Our next session will consider Chapters 50-53.

Our quiet moments for this reading may not be quite as intense as in previous weeks. However, these bends in the road will demand the same honesty and attention. We will begin to clarify some of the challenges of healing. What do we envision as we look forward?

OPPORTUNITY FOR GROWTH: In our next section of reading, we will be encouraged to look at suffering in a new way. (Chapter 50) We will also invite something into our discussion that, perhaps, we have been waiting for—hope. Yet, didn't we experience pain in the first place because our hopes were destroyed or abused? So, what is hope? Where do we find it? (Chapters 51–52) Can hope be beautiful again? (Chapter 53)

COURAGE AND PEACE:

We have acknowledged suffering as a natural, expected, and unavoidable part of life. This is a difficult concept to accept, and your heart may still be wrestling with it. Yet, you are healing—one step, one bend, at a time. And there *is* hope.

> God did this so that . . . we who have fled to take hold of the
> hope set before us may be greatly encouraged. We have this hope
> as an anchor for the soul, firm and secure. (Hebrews 6:18–19)

CLOSING

A NEW SONG BOOK STUDY
SESSION 8

CHAPTERS 50–53

Seeing Suffering In A New Way
Hope
Hope Realized
The Beauty Of Hope That Does Not Disappoint

INTENTIONS: To courageously look at suffering in a new way
To discern the difference between hoping and wishing
To acknowledge and accept the only true source of hope
To give a brief introduction to the Opportunity For Growth in Session 9

GREETING: This will be unique and personal to each group.

REFLECTION: There are few people who actually tackle the questions that we have been contemplating over the past weeks: "Why?" "Why me?" "Why this?" "How can pain result in good?" We did not settle all of our doubts or reveal all of the answers, but we did discover some footholds that will help us to continue on our forward journey. In particular, we discovered a God of ALL, who hears our questions and is with us in our pain. And we are stronger—and less vulnerable—because of the conversation.

OVERVIEW OF CHAPTERS FOR THIS SESSION: We began this reading with an invitation to see suffering in a new light—to see that "as much as we run from it and protect ourselves from it, suffering is not the bad guy." To see suffering this way takes some rearrangement in our thinking, but it is through this awareness that we can begin to embrace hope.

It's difficult to define the concept of hope, primarily because it is often misused. We confuse it with wishful thinking. So, Susan defines hope not as a verb—but as a noun. We do not "hope" for things; that is mere wishing. But we do place our hope *in* something—in someone. In the book of Exodus, we learn that this someone is God, who calls Himself "I Am." He alone is faithful, dependable, and worthy of our hope.

INVITATION TO SHARE: Let's consider this new look at suffering. Then we will attempt to clarify our expectations of hope.

1. (Chapter 50) Look at the "Suffering is . . . " list. Which of these possibilities can you connect with? Or which possibility are you going to contemplate through the next weeks of healing? Which item on this list seems the most challenging?

2. (Chapter 51) Many of us are in pain because our hopes were crushed, despised, or broken. This does not mean that these hopes were bad or unreasonable. It means that the object of our hope was flawed and undependable. What hopes did you have for life, relationships, and events that have been left unfulfilled, at least in the way you expected them to be?

3. (Chapter 52) Two pivotal points in moving forward include (1) putting boundaries around the hope that we so easily give to things and people that cannot possibly carry out that responsibility and (2) embracing I Am as our one and only dependable hope. Where are you in the process of applying these practices to your life? What do you find challenging?

PREFACE TO UPCOMING READING: Our next session will consider Chapters 54–59.

The majority of our journey to this point has focused on our pain, our crisis moments, and our responses. However, we all know that we are not the only people in our stories. There are those who suffered *with* us, perhaps even experiencing the same event but from a different vantage point. There may also be those who caused or added to our suffering.

This will not be an easy part of the journey. Yet, we are here, once again faced with hard work. Some of us may feel leery, as many of the topics brought to light so far may have seemed threatening. And so it is with courage that we must allow ourselves to be vulnerable, reminding ourselves of the discovery that we have made about this openness: it actually strengthens us and removes some of the control of the pain.

OPPORTUNITY FOR GROWTH: As we read the next chapters, we will consider others who belong to our stories and discuss the importance of remembering that each person's healing journey is different.

(Chapter 54) We will also talk about coming to peace with the kind of relationship we will have with those who caused or added to our suffering. We can choose to respond to these relationships in various ways: with denial, revenge, or bitterness—or, of course, with the always recommended forgiveness. In order to even consider forgiveness as an option, however, we must understand what it really means—including what it does not mean. (Chapters 56–57)

Then follows a chapter that nudges against the feeling of waste and ruin—the feeling that those years of suffering were spoiled. What do we do with those connections, moments, and opportunities that now seem tainted? To answer this question, we must consider another: Can anything be reclaimed? (Chapter 58)

The final portion of our reading might be unexpected. Susan once again invites us into her personal experience, which she describes as "a different kind of suffering." Perhaps, you will connect with this experience. (Chapter 59)

COURAGE & PEACE:

Here we are, well into our journey.
We have encountered multiple bends in the road, discovering truth,
gathering awareness of value, discarding deception.
Some things we hold close as a treasure,
others we have left on the roadside.
Sorting things out.
Unraveling.
Resolving.
Not one of us would describe this path as easy.
Yet, even with the intensity,
there is a sense of relief that is growing "slowly by slowly."
We are becoming familiar with our suffering,
gaining perspective of good and evil,
writing a new narrative that includes beauty.
And there is an awareness that we are, in fact, moving through healing,
as fear moves closer to courage, vulnerability gives way to strength,
and despair encounters hope.
(Chapter 60 page 261)

CLOSING

A NEW SONG BOOK STUDY
SESSION 9

CHAPTERS 54–59

Others In My Story
Those Who Caused The Pain
What About Forgiveness?
Forgiveness As A Part Of Resolution
Reclaimed
A Different Kind Of Suffering

INTENTIONS: To consider others who shared our experience
To honestly confront our responses to those who caused our hurt
To gain a clear understanding of what forgiveness is and what it is not
To open our hands to God's ability to reclaim things in our lives for good
To expose disobedience that has caused hurt in our lives
To comprehend our need for reconciliation with God
To give a brief introduction to the Opportunity For Growth in Session 10

GREETING: This will be unique and personal to each group.

REFLECTION: During our last session, we talked about hope. We concluded that much of what we do when we "hope" is actually just to "wish." That would be depressing if we ended the conversation there. However, we went on to discuss a different kind of hope—one that completely meets our expectations, lives up to our dreams, and holds true when everything else falls apart. Because of this sure hope, we can embrace the possibility of *good* in suffering. All of these concepts weave together to give guidance and encouragement on our healing journey.

OVERVIEW OF CHAPTERS FOR THIS SESSION: The reading for this session was fairly intense. If we opened our hearts in vulnerability, it might even have been a bit disturbing. Forward movement is sometimes like that.

We discussed how those who suffered with us need freedom to follow their own journeys of healing, as theirs might not be the same as ours or might not happen on the same timetable. So, we cannot expect our journeys to stay in sync. And then there are those who caused or added to our pain—what do we do with them? We are encouraged in the Bible not to seek vengeance—it never turns out well, and we are not good at it. Releasing our desire for retribution to God, however, brings unexpected peace.

Next, Susan opened the inevitable conversation about forgiveness. We looked at what forgiveness is and what it is not. Maybe you were surprised to find out that forgiveness and restoration are not always a package deal.

Finally, it was wonderful to end with the truth that many of the things we see as wasted in our lives can actually be reclaimed. We have much to talk about, so let's get started.

INVITATION TO SHARE:

1. (Chapter 54) What about others? Not the ones who caused the pain, but those who suffered with you or are connected to your story. Are you willing to release them to walk their own paths—at their own speed, and with their own emotional intensity? How might that help your relationship with others and bring peace to your expectations?

2. (Chapter 55) There is another type of relationship that needs attention: How do we respond to those who have harmed us? Your first bend in the road was to consider honestly what kind of justice you long for. (Chapter 56) And then came the conversation of forgiveness—what forgiveness is and what forgiveness is not. It is only when we have a clear depiction of forgiveness that we can actually consider how it might come to reality in our own situations. What clarifications about forgiveness were beneficial to you?

3. (Chapter 57) "Forgiveness is not identified by forgetfulness, but is evidenced by release. Forgiveness is not proven by restoration, but is perceptible by peace. Forgiveness is not something you give, but something you embrace." Did any part of these statements or anything from the overall conversation help you move forward with your own willingness, intention, or decision to embrace forgiveness? Where are you in that conversation with yourself?

4. (Chapter 58) *Wasted. Tainted.* These words haunt us when we consider some past events. Can you share how God has reclaimed such an event or something else in your life?

5. (Chapter 59) "Upheaval. Uncertainty. Disobedience. Only God Himself can provide a way for the relationship with Him to be healed. That restoration and healing only come through Jesus Christ." This chapter may have been unexpected, but it came from Susan's firsthand experience. She learned that areas of her relationship with God needed healing—and once those areas were addressed, it contributed to her overall healing and sense of well-being. Were you able to connect with this personally? Did you find encouragement in knowing that we can release our burdens of failure or disobedience?

PREFACE TO UPCOMING READING: Our next session will consider Chapters 60–65.

For those of you who resonate with tangible *how-tos*, the next chapters will be gratifying.

This contemplative journey is pressing you forward in ways you might not even recognize. For instance, at each bend in the road, you have encountered a challenge. You have considered the information presented and then, in some form or another, you have responded to questions such as, "Do I see this guidance as truth? Am I willing to accept the invitation, embrace the suggestions, and apply the conclusions in my own life?" And then, there is the clean-up: once we identify untruth, we must remove it. We are about to discover one of our strongest tools for healing—*the ability to remove untruth and, in its place, establish truth.* (Chapter 63 page 273)

OPPORTUNITY FOR GROWTH: We are encouraged by freedom and forward movement. Yet, we need something to keep us within certain boundaries of security. We need some safety tethers. These tethers can go with us anywhere and be available at any time. (Chapter 61) We can also think of our lives like a garden that needs tending. Susan will help us discover the threats to our gardens as well as the boundaries we need to put in place to protect our well-being. (Chapters 62–65)

COURAGE AND PEACE: "The LORD will guide you always; he will satisfy your needs in a sun-scorched land and will strengthen your frame. You will be like a well-watered garden, like a spring whose waters never fail." (Isaiah 58:11)

CLOSING

A NEW SONG BOOK STUDY
SESSION 10

CHAPTERS 60–65

Well Into Our Journey
Tethers
I Need
Truth And Untruth In Our Garden
Discovering The Need For Protection
Setting Boundaries

INTENTIONS: To identify the unshakeable tethers that keep us stable when we feel unsettled
To identify a physical tether that can help ground us
To discern truth and untruth
To create boundaries of protection for our garden of well-being
To give a brief introduction to the Opportunity For Growth in Session 11

GREETING: This will be unique and personal to each group.

REFLECTION: The themes in our previous section of reading were not for the faint-hearted: forgiveness, resolution, reclaiming the "wasted and tainted" parts of our lives. We talked about how the actions of others have affected our lives and brought suffering. Then we acknowledged how our own actions can contribute to our suffering. The reassuring conclusion helped us see that God is a perfect companion on our journey. For all the pain and uncertainty of other relationships and events, we can have peace with our Creator. We can experience the profound awareness of His mercy and grace and presence with us on every part of the journey.

OVERVIEW OF CHAPTERS FOR THIS SESSION: Even as we feel release and freedom, we want and need tethers that will hold us in a safe place. These tethers connect us to God because we continue to see that He is the only completely dependable component of our life.

It is also helpful to visualize life as a garden that needs our care and protection. With this visual in mind, we can remember the following:

- Truth and untruth cannot grow agreeably in the same garden, without one losing its influence and the other gaining control.

- We need boundaries around our garden, because strength, inspiration, and courage can *leak out*, while negative thoughts and accusations *intrude in*. Threats to our well-being can be real or perceived, but all are dangerous.

- Time and emotions, coping behavior, and relationships are three big areas around which we need to set realistic and reasonable boundaries.

- Our boundaries are not intended to keep us from all pain or discomfort, and to believe such would be wishful thinking! Rather, boundaries are meant to protect us from attacks that will overwhelm us or take us to a point of despair.

Our time of sharing will be good for us.

INVITATION TO SHARE:

1. (Chapter 61) Let's look together at the image of the strong tethers that can hold us and protect us. Which of these tethers do you identify with most? Which ones give assurance? Were you able to choose a physical connection for when the panic and fear set in?

2. (Chapter 63) We are often being bombarded by information and expectations. As such, untruth can quickly take root in the garden of our well-being—and before we know it, we have conflict. We had an opportunity to note specific truths and untruths that currently might be trying to co-exist in our garden. Are there any such pairs that you would be willing to share with us?

3. (Chapter 64) Susan helped us to start identifying areas in our life that need protection. Were you able to identify any threats, dangers, or untruth that are disturbing your well-being? What about any beauty, good, and truth that might be leaking?

4. (Chapter 65) Once we are aware of the need for boundaries, we want to put them in place with discernment. Was this idea of boundaries new to you? Were you glad to be given "permission" to put boundaries in place? Let's consider the three categories that Susan mentioned: time and emotions, coping behavior, and relationships. Without giving more details than would be appropriate (concerning other people, in particular), let's talk about our intentions for boundaries.

PREFACE TO UPCOMING READING: Our next session will consider Chapters 66–72.

We are taking steps forward. Some are more difficult than others, however, and eventually we are bound to encounter the challenge of change. Ideas, intentions, ways of thinking, and even our vocabulary will need to be reorganized, redesigned, and refashioned.

OPPORTUNITY FOR GROWTH: The first chapter for this reading confronts how we speak to ourselves. Perhaps a change in vocabulary is necessary. (Chapter 66)

Next, Susan shares from her personal experience to gently warn us about some of the possibilities on our journey—often, negative possibilities. We discover that we are not alone, however, and that there is a way forward. (Chapters 67–70)

Chapter 71 provides a hands-on way to visualize where we are "along the way."

Finally, we may encounter a challenge as we attempt to think beyond the immediate moment—beyond survival. Although this is natural, we will find that, with practice, we can learn to look up and forward with some degree of confidence. (Chapter 72)

COURAGE AND PEACE: Weeks ago, you were uncertain about how this journey would unfold. Even now, not everything is known or resolved. Yet, here you are, identifying threats, considering boundaries, speaking truth to yourself. You have shown courage. You have confronted difficult choices. By taking back control from trauma, you have become more capable of moving forward with hope. And by removing untruth and speaking to yourself in a language of encouragement, compassion, and truth, you are sowing peace.

CLOSING

A NEW SONG BOOK STUDY
SESSION 11

CHAPTERS 66–72

A New Vocabulary
The Reality of Fear
RE-
Those Moments
The Unexpected
Along The Way
Beyond The Next Step

INTENTIONS: To identify vocabulary that is harmful to us and

To correct the way we speak to ourselves

To acknowledge fear

To find reassurance

To courageously reorganize, redesign, and refashion areas that are no longer healthy

To be aware that moments of despair or anxiousness may still come

To creatively and honestly see and identify the ups and downs of our journey

To include the future in our thoughts, our conversations, and our plans

To give a brief introduction to the Opportunity For Growth in Session 12

GREETING: This will be unique and personal to each group.

REFLECTION: The truths we are gathering give us stability, so that we will not be easily thrown off balance. The tethers that are holding us are attached to God in a loving way, different from any other attachment we have experienced. The vague expectation to take control of our lives is daunting, but seeing our lives as a garden that we can plant, till, and protect unlocks the possibility for sowing truth and protecting ourselves from destructive hazards.

OVERVIEW OF CHAPTERS FOR THIS SESSION: As we have traveled this journey, each of us has come to know ourselves better and to recognize our own voice—including our self-encouragements and self-accusations. In the process, we might have discovered that our very own words were adding to the destruction, that our conversations with ourselves were feeding the trauma, which then integrated into every part of our lives. So, to address these destructive words and conversations, we had a vocabulary lesson. We took time to identify positive shifts in how we speak to ourselves. We also identified damaging words and phrases that are still in use and provided constructive replacements.

Next, we talked about fear. We discussed how, in our forward movement, we have many times attempted to regain the courage to see the good things in life— but that sometimes, fear unexpectedly swoops in and threatens those attempts. Many times, that fear is a reasonable response, but even then, we discovered that we can continue to move forward, through the fear—and when we do, we find ourselves faced with the task of reorganizing, redesigning, and refashioning. We also find ourselves faced with the choice of how to react to the new insight and awareness that come: we can accuse ourselves or we can accept it as wisdom, which enables us to move forward in a healthier way.

We have been reminded often on this journey that coming to peace with suffering is not a straight line; it involves moments of victory followed by unexpected and uninvited moments that leave us shaken. But we have also learned to welcome ways to express ourselves in those moments, both positive and negative. So, in the last portion of our reading, we were introduced to yet another way to assess and express where we are on our journey—images that helped us see ourselves and our progress. These little figures helped us to speak or perhaps even cry out for help. They also encouraged us to recognize where we may be stuck spiraling for a time or where we might be making forward movement.

And what does that forward movement look like? For so long, many of us have had difficulty looking up from our feet—beyond the immediate or beyond survival. So, in the final chapter of reading for this session, we discussed what moving forward might look like in our everyday lives, and we acknowledged that it may be time to consider what is beyond.

INVITATION TO SHARE:

1. (Chapter 66) What have you noticed in your conversations with yourself? Have there been shifts in how you encourage, discourage, speak truth, or correct untruth? Are there ways you speak to yourself that still need to be corrected?

2. (Chapter 67) We are often told we should not fear. And yet, there it is—we feel it. What did you discover about yourself and fear? What assurance can you use as a shield when fear and uncertainty surround you?

3. (Chapter 68) We cannot take this journey without making necessary changes. What need do you see to reorganize, redesign, refashion—in particular—your responses to pain, guilt, difficult circumstances?

4. (Chapter 69) Susan described one of "those moments" in this chapter and then reassured us by saying, "I tell you this because I don't want you to be alarmed when it happens to you. I don't want you to feel disappointment and failure. I don't know where or when—but it will happen." Is there anything you would like to share about "those moments" in your life? Was it helpful to know that you are not the only one?

5. (Chapter 72) "Eyes on floor, eyes on feet, foot lifts, body moves forward . . . repeat." You may have felt the challenge of lifting your eyes toward the future. Are you able to look toward the future, a future that includes things other than the survival of your suffering? A future that includes the positive, hope, and life?

6. (Chapter 71) These little figures might have been a new experience for you. They do help us see ourselves more clearly. Who would like to use these images to express a part of your journey—in the past, along the way, or currently?

PREFACE TO UPCOMING READING: Our next session will consider Chapters 73–77.

Up to this point, we have become familiar with suffering and the trauma that can follow. We have also made changes and decisions that have helped us to regain our confidence and release the hold that suffering had on us. Now, as we go forward, it will be important to know what to plant in the places where we uprooted untruth. Therefore, our final group of chapters will provide seeds that you can plant that will grow strong along our pathway. It feels good to plant. And it will feel good to anticipate new fruit.

OPPORTUNITY FOR GROWTH: Could it be that joy and peace can flourish once again—or for the first time? (Chapters 73; 76-77)

Is there a way to protect our hearts and to live into the future with anticipation rather than dread? And how do we face the possibility of new pain? (Chapter 74-75)

COURAGE AND PEACE: We began our journey weeks ago, wondering if there was any possibility of hearing music again—if there was truly any way forward. Then as we made our way along the path, we found ourselves encountering truth and beauty and hope. At times, we have felt weak, but we have been continuously reassured that . . .

> those who hope in the LORD will renew their strength.
>
> They will soar on wings like eagles;
>
> they will run and not grow weary,
>
> they will walk and not be faint. (Isaiah 40:31)

Next, we will ponder the expectation of peace and joy:

> May the God of hope
>
> fill you with all joy and peace
>
> as you trust in him,
>
> so that you may overflow with hope. (Romans 15:13)

Yes, the music is beginning.

CLOSING

PARTICIPANT END-OF-STUDY TESTAMENT ACTIVITY

"I CAME IN" / "I AM GOING OUT"

(Give to participants after Session 11 in preparation for Session 12

> Present this activity in the next-to-last session to help participants prepare for the final session.
>
> Give each person a piece of paper or cardstock (3x5 or 4x6 is suggested, but any size will do) and ask them to write the title on the card (see instructions below). Alternatively, you could title the cards beforehand and distribute them at the end of Session 11.
>
> This assignment is a bit difficult to think about quickly and with clarity in the moment, so the idea is to give participants time to ponder and to come prepared to talk about it during your last session.

We are always looking for ways to express where we are on this journey—to assess our status. But "How do you feel?" is too big of a question. So let's focus in on just some of the shifts that we have observed in ourselves so far—changes, parts of us that have been reclaimed, or just some new descriptive of how we see ourselves.

Some of you may have a difficult time seeing or speaking about the positives you have observed over the previous weeks. Often, we hesitate to acknowledge or speak about the positives—especially to others—for fear that it means we are somehow saying that all is now fine. But it is important that you allow yourself to see how you were as you came into this group and then to adjust that view, to see the progress you have made during our time together. Yes, you *have* taken steps forward.

We are going to use this card to record a testament to our growth:

On one side: On the other side:

I CAME IN:	*I AM GOING OUT:*

Use the time before our next session to consider with honesty and compassion what changes you see—or sense—in yourself. Think about your emotions, your state of mind, your sense of well-being. We all know we are not at the end of our journey, so we should avoid contrasts like "I came in: suffering"/"I am going out: healed." But as you look carefully in the mirror, so to speak, there are contrasts that are there. It may take time, but you will find answers to these questions if you look long enough:

How would you describe yourself when you first walked into this group?

What is different, new, changed, reclaimed as you walk out of the group?

Take this card with you and spend some time to think on these things. We will have opportunity to share during our final session.

We have learned that the pathway to resolution is not a straight line. But there is clear forward movement. We see it in ourselves and we see it in each other. So, together, we will give testimony to that growth. And these testimonies will be some of the melodies in our new song.

A NEW SONG BOOK STUDY
FINAL SESSION 12

CHAPTERS 73–77

PEACE?
MY GUARDED HEART
HOW DO WE NOW LIVE?
LET THERE BE JOY
YOUR NEW SONG

INTENTIONS: To understand that peace is not the absence of conflict
To understand that our peace is directly related to our understanding of God
To embrace a way of life that leads to peace
To understand the importance of guarding the heart
To comprehend the expanse of life beyond the cradle and the grave
To gain confidence for the life *between,* from the understanding of life beyond
To open the heart and emotion to the possibility of joy
To listen for and recognize the sound of a new song

GREETING: This will be unique and personal to each group.

REFLECTION: In the past session, we looked honestly at the path of healing, including the changes and the challenges. As we did, it seemed that our journey somehow weaved in and out of past, present, and future. After many bends in the road, we are now coming to peace with suffering. We are even coming to a point where we can consider opening our hearts to the possibility of *good* in the future. And with that, we come to our last discussion of the final chapters.

OVERVIEW OF CHAPTERS FOR THIS SESSION: Here we are, considering the possibility of peace, of joy, of music! This conversation is evidence that we are further along the road than when we began weeks ago. We are still not looking for a finish line, however. Neither are we measuring the distance we have come. But we are clearly aware that some things have changed or been rearranged. Untruth has been uprooted, and in its place, we are planting seeds that promise to grow a new and positive perspective of suffering that will flow into other areas of our lives. We are coming to peace.

What is peace? We know that peace goes beyond the presence or absence of conflict. Peace settles *down in* and also wells *up from*. Peace is a particular awareness of God who is present and holds control over the seeming chaos around us. Peace is also a way of life that we can choose.

One aspect of that peace that we discussed in this reading was the necessity to guard our hearts—in a sense, to put boundaries around them. Gaining an understanding of how to guard our hearts is a turning point in learning how to move forward in a healthy way. We need this understanding to help us with our past, present, and future.

As we consider looking beyond the next step, however, will understanding and knowledge be enough? In other words, knowing what we now *know*, how do we now *live*? There is no formula. Rather, the truths that we have absorbed will sway us toward new responses, reclaimed and redesigned—and this includes our response to the idea of joy.

We often push joy aside because we are afraid that it sends out messages that we *don't* mean: *I am healed. The pain is over. The betrayal is forgotten.* In reality, joy means none of those things. Joy means only that we can welcome good things into our life again—because the suffering is not consuming us as it once did.

So, could there actually be a song? We can be witnesses of the new beginnings we see in each other — witnesses of the evidence that we are moving toward healing. Let me give you some examples: we are speaking with more courage; we are not running from the expression of emotion; we are setting shame aside and embracing reassurance and resolution; we are finding the ability to open our eyes to the big picture—because our focus is not as consumed by the pain; we are discovering our identity and taking back some control. Let's give voice to these steps toward healing and many more. These are the notes that will form the melodies of our new songs. So, let's talk about these final chapters that encourage us forward.

INVITATION TO SHARE:

> As you plan your timing for this section, remember that you want to allow time for sharing from the "I came in/I am going out" card given at the close of your previous session.

1. (Chapter 73) Peace is sometimes difficult to describe. We long for it, and yet it seems elusive. Susan gave us some good descriptives of peace, along with suggestions for how to pursue peace in practical ways. What do you think—is it possible? Can you make some adjustments, so that peace can abide more fully—even when there is conflict around you? What was encouraging or challenging to you in this chapter?

2. (Chapter 74) Our hearts lead us forward—into good places and into dangerous places. God knows that our hearts need to be guarded in many ways to protect us from ourselves. What did you learn about your own heart? What areas need protection? How was this conversation good for you as you care for yourself?

3. (Chapter 75) We might wish otherwise, but we know there is more pain, more suffering, more loss in the future. Was there anything that particularly resonated with you in Susan's description in this chapter of how we can prepare to face our unknown future?

4. (Chapter 76) "Do not be afraid of joy. Your joy is not a betrayal of the suffering. Joy is part of your new song." Are you beginning to accept joy in a way that you have avoided previously? What are some expressions of joy that you are beginning to feel in your life?

5. (Chapter 77) We have mentioned the anticipation of hearing and singing a new song. This anticipation is evidence of renewed purpose, identity, and awareness of your value. Let's share some ways that this new song is becoming evident in our lives. It might not be a full song yet—but can you hear the introduction? Let's take this time to share from the cards you received at our last session: I came in/I am going out.

How would you describe yourself when you first walked into this group?

What is different, new, changed, reclaimed as you walk out of the group?

| I CAME IN: | I AM GOING OUT: |

OPPORTUNITY FOR GROWTH: What opportunities for growth are in front of us? Let's listen to how Susan brings our time to a close: (Read Chapter 77 aloud.)

COURAGE AND PEACE:

Your path is unique.

Take time to ponder the blessings and the challenges . . .

the joy and the suffering . . .

the bright hues and the dark shades.

Avoid not one bend in the road.

All weave the exquisite tapestry of your life

with perfect design.

OPPORTUNITY FOR RESPONSE

Dear group leaders,

Thank you for coming alongside me and the participants of your group. It is not a coincidence that you are here right now. Not one of us can heal or reclaim a story, but together we can gently turn faces and spirits toward the One who *can*.

This book and the leader's guide are more than an offering of information or the foundation for another study. They are an out-held hand to both participant and leader. They are an offering of companionship and shared courage. As such, our connection does not end with your purchase of the book and your participation in the study. I would love to hear from you.

It would be helpful to hear about your experience of leading and to get your recommendations and your thoughts about the study in the lives of the participants you worked with. ,

I would also love to hear from the participants about moments they experienced, whether of awareness, truth, challenge, or reclamation. Encourage them to use the questions in the back of the book as a springboard to that sharing. They may use the email address given there to respond to me personally.

Feel free to use the questions below this letter to open your own conversation with me. You may email your responses to susan@susanhabeggerauthor.com.

Each response is a valuable part of someone's story and a treasure to be protected. Thank you in advance for your trust.

Together, I believe that these connections will build a network of courage, peace, and strength.

With gratitude,

Susan

As a leader:

- ❄ How did the leader's guide help prepare you for the logistics and challenges of leading a group?
- ❄ How did the session guides help with your in-the-moment experience of leading each session?
- ❄ What would have added to your preparation or support in this experience?

As a leader on the healing journey:

- ❄ What was challenging about leading others while taking your own journey of healing?
- ❄ What moments of truth opened a door toward healing in a particular area of your pain?

As a protector of others' stories:

- ❄ In what ways did you observe participants gain courage and/or peace through this study?
- ❄ What changes took place in your group through the weeks, as relationships formed?
- ❄ How did the participants respond as they came to the conclusion of your time together?

If this book has benefited you on your journey of healing or in your desire to help others on that journey, I would appreciate a short review on Amazon.com, so that other readers might benefit from your words and from this book.

ABOUT THE AUTHOR

Susan Habegger, founder and director of Thrive Life Skills, an international ministry organization, has lived and worked for over 30 years with suffering people around the world, but not until she unexpectedly met suffering firsthand did her thoughts on healing transform, inspiring her to write *A New Song*. Susan lives with her daughter and family in Michigan, where she explores the Lake Michigan shores. Her constant companion, at home or traveling, is her Good Shepherd.

The conversations in *A New Song* are excellent topics for Conferences, Workshops, and Retreats. To request Susan as speaker, go to susanhabeggerauthor.com for more information.

www.ingramcontent.com/pod-product-compliance
Lightning Source LLC
Chambersburg PA
CBHW082109120626
46553CB00011B/3604